W9-AOV-980

THE PASTA QUEEN

THE PASTA QUEEN

A Just Gorgeous Cookbook

100+ RECIPES AND STORIES

Nadia Caterina Munno

WITH KATIE PARLA

GALLERY BOOKS

New York   London   Toronto   Sydney   New Delhi

Gallery Books
An Imprint of Simon & Schuster, Inc.
1230 Avenue of the Americas
New York, NY 10020

Copyright © 2022 by Nadia Caterina Munno
Illustrations by Dorota Sosnówka
Food and portrait photography by Giovanna Di Lisciandro
Lifestyle photography by Stef Galea

Page xv, top left, photo courtesy of the author
Pages xx–xxi photos courtesy of Pastificio Di Martino
Page xxiv photo courtesy of Officine Gullo

First Gallery Books hardcover edition November 2022

GALLERY BOOKS and colophon are registered
trademarks of Simon & Schuster, Inc.

For information about special discounts for
bulk purchases, please contact Simon & Schuster
Special Sales at 1-866-506-1949
or business@simonandschuster.com.

The Simon & Schuster Speakers Bureau can bring
authors to your live event. For more information or
to book an event, contact the Simon & Schuster
Speakers Bureau at 1-866-248-3049 or visit our
website at www.simonspeakers.com.

Manufactured in China

10 9 8 7 6 5 4 3 2 1

Library of Congress Cataloging-in-Publication
data is available.

ISBN 978-1-9821-9515-1
ISBN 978-1-9821-9516-8 (ebook)

For my mother, Kathleen, Nonna Caterina, Zia Pina, Zia Stella, Angela, and Nonna Michelina, my inspirations in the kitchen and in life.

CHAPTER ONE
PASTA BASICS

CHAPTER TWO
WHERE IT ALL BEGAN
The Classics

CHAPTER THREE
BE MY GUEST
Recipes to Impress

To my brother,
Agostino. My inseparable
best friend.

MY STORY
Where It All Started

It was early 2020, just before the world imploded. One night, my daughter Desiree showed me a new dancing app on her phone, which I was convinced was called "ticky-tock." After about ten swipes of watching a girl named Charli dance and people making videos to sounds from the Kardashians' reality show, I sighed and was done. My water was boiling downstairs and I needed to gather basil leaves from the garden to prepare my family's favorite meal, Pasta with Pesto alla Genovese.

As I was about to walk out of Desiree's room, I heard a woman onscreen announce that she was going to show us how to make the perfect lasagna. I turned back around: "Okay—you've got my attention. Let's see how the perfect lasagna is made." I had no expectations, just intrigue.

The woman's recipe began with a premade beef sauce, which was gray with a thick layer of oily water on top. This strange liquid was drained into a baking tray, and bright-yellow plastic-like pasta sheets were placed on top. As I watched I became increasingly agitated, but couldn't place why. This was none of my business. Why did I care what this woman was making on ticky-tock?

Next, a strange cheese was peeled out of a plastic film. It was a rich luminescent orange, glowing like the sun, and it was placed on top of the pasta sheets. I flinched. I was usually okay with anyone cooking whatever they thought was great. But this user was telling everyone that this was the perfect lasagna.

I left to go finish the pesto. As I was putting the fresh basil and pine nuts into the food processor, my mind was stuck on the image of that "lasagna." It was a moment of great personal reflection. I flashed back to my childhood, to the perfectly structured lasagnas we'd have, made from meat sauce, farm-fresh mozzarella, and homemade pasta sheets. With every bite, you'd feel a little bit more alive, and somehow the room would feel brighter, faces looked happier, and the sun grew warmer.

It's hard to describe how one feels when one finds their purpose in life. Over the next few days, my heart would race and my face would flush with excitement thinking about sharing *my* lasagna with the world. Goals were becoming clear to me. I wanted to bring my beautiful culture into the homes of others, and what better way to do it than by becoming an emissary of Italy and its simple, great food? It is faster to make a homemade sauce with fresh ingredients than to order takeout and food delivery. In fact, all you really need for a great meal are three pillars: love of self, love of others, and love of food. This can be accomplished by anyone. Yes—anyone.

And that is how The Pasta Queen began.

Pasta is my love language, and I've been speaking it for as long as I can remember. My love affair with pasta began shortly after I was born in Rome, where I learned to twirl spaghetti before I could even talk, and near Naples where, as a toddler, my *nonna* taught me the magic of making homemade pasta, gently guiding my tiny hands with the most tender affection and love. As soon as I could reach the stove, I learned to simmer broth for pastina for my brother, Agostino, wrapping his small hand around a spoon and teaching him how to eat every last drop.

I have always been fascinated by the world of pasta, and I cannot remember a time when I wasn't cooking it. I learned from the best, my Nonna Caterina, who had learned to cook from her grandmother, who had learned from her grandmother, and so on. I inherited this generational knowledge from spending countless hours in the kitchen with the women in my family, absorbing their secrets like pasta water absorbs Pecorino Romano in a perfect bowl of cacio e pepe. Like them, I have always been driven to cook for the people I care for, as I believe that cooking with fresh ingredients is the purest expression of love. And now I want to share my love—my rich culinary history and my family's recipes, before this known only to the Munno family—with you.

I may have been born in Rome, but my family originally comes from the south of Italy, the land of gorgeous gladiators and pasta gods. The Munnos were dried pasta makers stretching back to the 1800s. I spent the first five years of my life, and then almost every summer after, in a village near Naples called Santa Maria Capua Vetere in the region of Campania, home to the stone amphitheater where Spartacus trained and began his legendary rebellion against the Romans. This ancient town is equally famous among Italians as a place where the locals harvested grain and made dried pasta in small family businesses to support themselves.

My family was dedicated to making pasta and farming the land in the amphitheater's shadow. We harvested grain from the fertile, nearly black volcanic soil of the area, milling it into a fine white powder and mixing it with mineral-rich water from the local springs to make the world's best dried pasta. Pasta making wasn't just our job, it was our life. It was an absolute passion for us, and we celebrated it daily—grandparents, aunts, uncles, and cousins packed around the table, trading stories and gossip over heaping plates of perfectly al dente pasta. And all along, each generation made its food from the land, growing everything they ate, right down to the grains to make flour for pasta. This precious gold is the tapestry into which my family's history is woven, and that serves as my daily muse in the kitchen today.

My family's roots to the land form some of my most precious memories. When I was young, my grandparents Caterina and Agostino would take me to their fields for the grain harvest in the peak of summer. The tiny, precious wheat berries were collected lovingly and spread on large sheets to dry in the heat. Agostino and I would dive into the warm piles of sunbathing wheat berries and swim through the sea of fragrant grain, loosening the fluffy bran that would billow around us and stick to our skin. Nonno Agostino would ruffle our hair as a playful punishment, sending bran swirling around us once again.

The dried wheat berries were milled into white flour that we sold to the local pasta collective to make dough to create shapes that are some of my favorites to this day—spaghetti, ziti, penne, candele. All this happened on a street in Santa Maria Capua Vetere that locals still call Maccheroni Street, because of the dozens of small, family-run factories that once buzzed with activity and a passion for pasta. When we walk down the street, neighbors still shout "*Maccheroni*," the Munno family nickname, to get our attention.

The factory is unfortunately closed, but the memory lives on. So do the lessons shared with my brother and me by my nonna and all the women in my family. The most precious? Whatever care you put into growing and making food, the land repays many times over with harvest and nourishment.

My mission in life is to share this lesson with the world through my family's amazing recipes, alongside those I have adapted or created myself. A couple of years ago, this seemed like an unlikely dream. Then I discovered TikTok and created an account called The Pasta Queen, pouring my pasta passion onto the screen. Within a few months I'd gained an audience with whom I had an instant, electric connection. Those first months were magical. People were making my recipes and my family's traditions were traveling the world. I was making good on my nonna's lessons, spreading the gospel of beautiful, genuine food made from scratch. Many of my followers told me I brought back the joy of cooking to their kitchens, or that I inspired them to skip fast food and takeout to make a nourishing plate of simple pasta instead. Others remarked that they found themselves spending more time savoring and enjoying their food rather than eating quickly and hurrying away from the table. All of this electrified me with pure happiness.

It truly feels as though together we are keeping my family's precious pasta traditions alive and building a bridge between their simple, agricultural past and the food we enjoy today. As you cook, you are beginning your very own journey, connected to mine, but very much your own. So what are you waiting for? Let's get started!

ABOUT THESE
Just Gorgeous RECIPES

Like my birth city of Rome, my collection of recipes wasn't built in a day. Every experience, relationship, and adventure I have had has shaped the way I cook, eat, and communicate love through food. Trust me when I tell you that it has been quite a journey! I want to take you on a tour through my life to share the recipes that have been important to me and that have defined me at each turn. You'll enjoy the recipes I learned as a young girl, to the meals that defined me as an adult—and later, a wife and mother—to the dishes that helped me become the Pasta Queen and, eventually, create this book. Along the way, I will teach you how to choose beautiful ingredients, find comfort in challenging times, and encourage you to build on my lessons to start your own journey to pasta mastery. Most of all, I want you to cook with intuition, as my nonna did and as she taught me. Of course I'm going to give you recipes. But I want these to be guides that give you the confidence to cook with your senses and with passion!

In the first chapter, Pasta Basics, I'll teach you how to make the fresh pasta doughs that I learned beside my nonna in her kitchen. In the next chapter, we will move through the classics, where I'll share traditional recipes for some of Italy's signature dishes, as well as the meals that nourished me during my childhood in Rome and Southern Italy. I'll recount my own love story in Chapter 3, which will help you fall in love with pastas you can make to impress your own lovers, friends,

family, or even yourself! In the fourth chapter, Family First, we'll make the quick and easy recipes that carried me through the glorious transition into motherhood, and that can help anyone balance delicious, homemade food with a tight schedule. We'll explore my family's move to America in the fifth chapter and learn how to make soothing meals that give strength and comfort during difficult times. And last, Pasta Renaissance, a collection of creative dishes that represent the culmination of all that I have learned during my journey as a woman, wife, mother, and TikTok's Pasta Queen. It will celebrate the *just gorgeous* recipes that went viral—all thanks to you!—when I shared them with you from the heart of my home, that virtual trattoria that is my kitchen. Throughout this journey, I will be holding your hand, guiding you as you cook and sharing all the knowledge I have inherited from my family and my Italian heritage.

Dried vs Fresh Pasta

The first chapter and some of the recipes that follow feature fresh pasta. But most of the book is a celebration of dried pasta, including many of the very shapes my family dutifully produced in their factory near Naples for generations. The truth is that Italians don't typically make fresh pasta every day, and that we love dried pasta just as much—and in my case, even more!—than fresh. Traditionally, Italians prepared fresh pasta for special occasions, holidays, and family gatherings. My family eats Tagliatelle al Ragù di Lady Caterina (page 62) on the weekends and Lasagna al Ragù di Lady Caterina (page 71) at Christmas, and I encourage you to make fresh pasta whenever your heart desires, though most of the recipes in the book call for dried pasta. Whether you choose fresh or dried, the dishes I share will make you fall in love with pasta and make you appreciate it more than you ever did before.

The Magic of Pasta Water

The book goes beyond recipes to share all my techniques and secret weapons for making flawless pasta dishes every time. Among the most important is harnessing the divine power of the "tears of the gods," aka starchy pasta water, which is absolutely essential for making the perfect pasta dish. As pasta dances in boiling water, it releases starch to create a cloudy elixir. Simmering the tears of the gods with sauce and cooked pasta concentrates the starches, which help bind the sauce to the pasta shape and creates a silky and smooth marriage of flavor and texture. You'll see that I rarely tell you to drain the pasta—pasta for cold salads and some baked dishes are the only exceptions—so you always have more than enough starchy magic on hand to finish your gorgeous recipes.

Salt

Another secret is salting. Adding salt to pasta water seasons the pasta, which contributes flavor to the finished product. You should add salt until the water tastes like a seasoned soup (that's about 4 tablespoons of salt per 6 quarts water, or 10 grams of salt and 1 liter of water for every 100 grams of pasta). Generally, though, I never measure salt and I don't think you should, either. Just add salt and taste the water as you go to get used to using and trusting your senses as you cook.

Salting while you cook is also the key to tasty food. I salt ingredients as I cook, tasting as I go to ensure that each ingredient is properly seasoned according to my taste. I also taste the pasta from the pan before plating it, adding a bit more salt if needed. I trust you to season the way you see fit, which is why I rarely list salt quantities, preferring you to get to know your ingredients and tastes in order to determine when the seasoning is just perfect.

Measurements

Almost all the recipes were written using US measurements, but the fresh pasta recipes use metric weights instead of volume, because that is more accurate when it comes to measuring flour. For example, 1 cup of flour may weigh 125 grams or 150 grams, depending on its freshness and humidity. A kitchen scale costs about $10 online, and it's one of the best investments you can make when it comes to homemade pasta. Use it so your dough recipe is consistent until you master it. Then, like an Italian, you can eyeball your ingredients, mixing and kneading dough according to the way it feels.

Dried Pasta Shapes

If you want to become a pasta master, you have to put in the time to get familiar with the various dried pasta shapes and how they behave. Three brands of spaghetti might have three very different cooking times, depending on how the pasta was made and how long it was dried in the factory. Quality artisanal pasta brands are dried slowly, which makes a pasta that cooks gorgeously. Meanwhile, big industrial brands dry the pasta with a blast of heat, which makes the product more brittle.

I recommend finding a brand you love (my favorites are listed in Resources, page 237) and getting to know its shapes intimately—the way the wheat flavor comes through when it cooks, what an al dente (see my definition, page xxii) piece of pasta feels like, and how a sauce clings to the shape (or doesn't) depending on

the pasta's geometry and the sauce's consistency. If unopened, dried pasta has a shelf life of about two years; once opened, it will keep in a well-sealed container for up to one year.

Most of the recipes in this book call for specific pasta shapes, but I also suggest alternate shapes that will pair well with the sauce, so you can choose one based on your preference. (The alternate fresh pastas can be either homemade from my recipes or store-bought.) The recipes are guidelines and not law! I want to provide you with a foundation so that you learn to trust you own instincts, create recipes that you adore, and feel free to cook with any pasta you wish!

As you cook, remember, the most precious ingredient is YOU. Trust yourself to season dishes to taste, select the best ingredients, and cook with confidence and love!

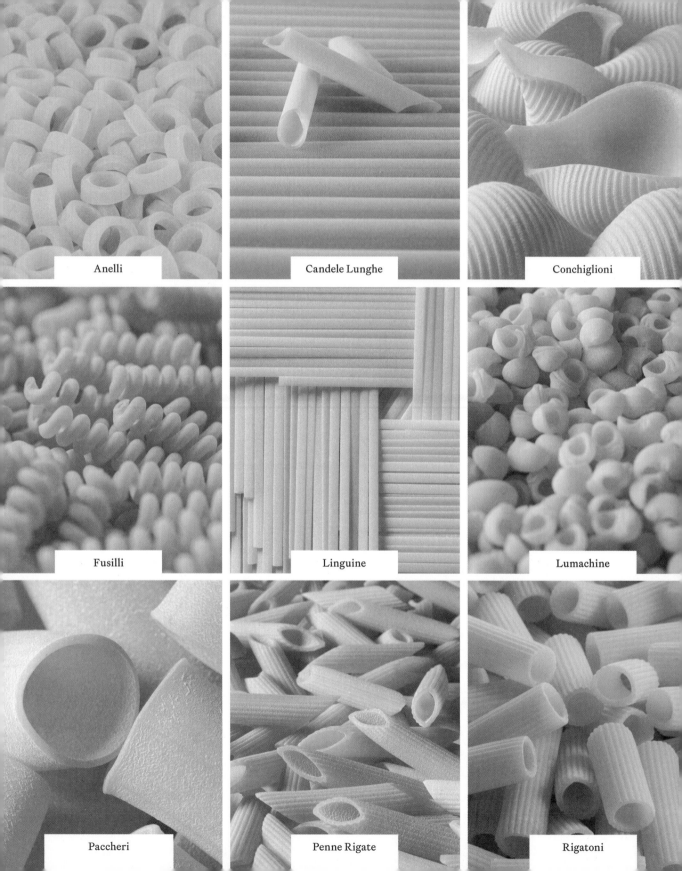

Anelli

Candele Lunghe

Conchiglioni

Fusilli

Linguine

Lumachine

Paccheri

Penne Rigate

Rigatoni

Ditali

Eliche Giganti

Fusillata Casareccia

Lumaconi

Mezzi Rigatoni

Mista Corta

Spaghetti

Spaghettoni

Trottole

PASTA QUEEN–*isms*

Cooking is all about emotion and instinct. Sense how your pasta should be seasoned, adopt techniques that will make the dish its most gorgeous, and feel when your pasta has been perfectly cooked. The best way to do this is also the most fun: Taste it frequently as it cooks! Here is my glossary of signature Pasta Queen terms, which I use throughout the book, to help get you there.

A HEAVY PINCH OF SALT: about a teaspoon

A PINCH OF SALT: ½ teaspoon

A LADLEFUL OF PASTA COOKING WATER: ½ cup

A SPLASH OF PASTA COOKING WATER: ¼ cup

A SCRUNCH OF PEPPER: For me, a scrunch of pepper is about ½ teaspoon, but the exact amount is very individual. Black pepper—which is best when it's ground fresh—can either be very strong and piquant or more subtle and understated, depending on the type of peppercorns you're using and how fresh they are. Use your senses to determine how much pepper you need to fully season your dish. That personal amount is your scrunch.

AL DENTE: Pasta or rice that is nearly cooked through, and that still has some bite to it when chewed. Al dente pasta also has a small amount of white inside when cut down the middle.

VERY AL DENTE: Pasta or rice that has been cooked for a little more than half the recommended cooking time (this will vary from shape to shape and brand to brand), and that is still hard and a bit crunchy when you bite into it. Very al dente pasta still has quite a bit of white inside when cut down the middle.

MANTECARE: A technique that emulsifies a pasta sauce by binding fat (oil, butter, cream, or a cheese-based sauce) with starchy cooking water (tears of the gods when pasta is involved), which happens when the two elements are mixed together energetically. This occurs at the end of the pasta cooking process when the pasta and sauce are combined and stirred together with passion. It is the stage in risotto making when the al dente rice is mixed enthusiastically with butter, oil, or cheese. Italian lesson alert! *Mantecare* is the Italian verb for "emulsify," and *mantecatura* is the act of emulsifying. Every risotto and almost every pasta sauce in this book is *mantecato*, meaning "emulsified."

THE TEARS OF THE GODS: My nickname for pasta water. One of the most magnificent experiences you can ever have in Rome—and this is saying a lot—is to be in the Pantheon when it rains. The building dedicated to the Roman gods has a hole in its dome, and it's such a magical and rare occasion to see raindrops falling through it. They are so precious that I've named starchy pasta cooking water, which acts like a glue to bind sauce to pasta, after them. When added to a simmering pasta sauce, the liquid evaporates, concentrating the starches in the sauce even more. It helps the mantecatura and makes an irresistible silky final product. Tears of the gods is the secret ingredient for any perfect pasta dish.

PASTA RISOTTATA: A pasta dish such as The Assassin's Spaghetti (page 195) or Lemon Temptress (page 213) that has been cooked in the style of risotto: adding small quantities of warm liquid to the pan as it cooks and until it is al dente.

PASTA MINESTRATA: A pasta dish such as Pastina in Brodo (page 138), Pasta e Fagioli (page 60), or The Lazy Princess (page 210) that is cooked entirely in its sauce, often in stock or broth.

KITCHEN TOOLS

A few kitchens have defined my cooking experience and, therefore, my life. The first was Nonna Caterina's, a place that was constantly bursting at the seams to accommodate dishes and tableware for the literally dozens of guests she would welcome every Sunday afternoon for lunch. Looking back, she really didn't have all that many tools—the ones she had were mostly for pasta—and they had been collected over a lifetime. She made the most brilliant meals with the few humble pots and pans that hung on her wall—some inherited, some purchased, but all with signs of loving use.

My first kitchen as an adult was small and bare-bones, with a malfunctioning stovetop and barely enough space for two people to stand comfortably. I don't really miss it, to be honest, but I am grateful for its lesson that you don't need much space to make a perfect pasta—only love. I was happy to leave the warped and threadbare pans behind when we moved into an apartment with a proper kitchen, but I know the pasta I prepared in that silly little cucina was some of the most soulful I have ever made.

My kitchen today is something I never could have dreamed of back when I was growing up. It's basically a mini restaurant in my own home, from which I broadcast my love of cooking to both my personal and Pasta Queen families. The center of it all is a tailor-made, ocean-blue stove from Italy. The room is filled with pots, pans, and pasta tools that I have collected over the course of my life, each with its own magic memory and story to tell. There's even a little area just for my youngest child, Penelope Dolce, to cook in! It is the absolute heart of my home and it is the sun that my family revolves around. Years before I joined social media and became the Pasta Queen, I knew I wanted a special place for sharing love and recipes, and I built it as a kind of premonition. Now it has become a virtual trattoria of sorts, where I invite people all over the world to share in my passion of cooking every day.

I hope that you have the kitchen of your dreams today or, if not, someday in the future, so you can make gorgeous meals for the ones you care for in a space you love. But know that with just a couple of burners, a few basic tools, and a whole lot of passion, you can make Pasta Queen–level meals no matter where you are. You probably already have most of what you need. Only a few recipes in this cookbook require special equipment, and I offer alternatives when possible. You can find all my favorite tools and kitchen accessories via the QR code in the Resources section (page 237). Here are some items that you do need:

Baking Dishes and Baking Sheets

Several of the baked pasta recipes in this book, like Radiatori al Forno (page 166) and Lasagna Vegetariana (page 136), were developed with standard 9 × 13-inch baking dishes. If you don't have a baking dish exactly that size, use what you have that can comfortably fit the pasta, and adjust the baking time accordingly. If you want to scale up a recipe for a party or to feed a large family, you can double up on the pans or use a larger dish. I personally love collecting large stainless-steel pans from restaurant supply stores for when I make lasagna for twenty. But in general, you don't need to run out and buy anything special; what you've already stocked your cupboards with should suit your needs. As for baking sheets, I use 18 × 13-inch half-sheet pans, which are large enough to accommodate ingredients—for example, when roasting mushrooms or squash for fresh pasta fillings.

Bowls

You will need small, medium, and large bowls for mixing. The material is up to you, but I generally use glass and stainless steel.

Cheese Grater

Many of my recipes call for finely grated Pecorino Romano or Parmigiano-Reggiano cheese. To get the perfect powdery consistency, I use the smallest punched holes of a box grater, which makes the cheese very fine for melting into sauces and for raining into the nooks and crannies of pasta after plating. A Microplane that grates very finely works well, too.

Food Mill

Use a food mill to remove tomato skins for Fresh Tomato Sauce (page 155).

Food Processors and Blenders

A food processor will make your pesto smooth, whip a bit of airy lightness into your ravioli fillings, and transform a portion of your soup into a silky contrast to the other ingredients. Blenders and immersion blenders will also give you smoothness that you can't get from hand mixing.

Fresh Pasta Tools

If you want to make fresh pasta, there are a few handy tools you can add to your arsenal such as a wooden pasta board and 2- to 3-foot-long rolling pins for rolling large disks of Sfoglia all'Uovo (page 9). I think wood, due to its warmth, is such a nice surface for pasta making. Pasta boards are designed to fit on your work surface, with a lip that overhangs the edge to prevent it from slipping. Another useful tool is a pasta machine that you can use to roll long rectangular pasta sheets. Most of the

time I make pasta dough with a rolling pin and a board, just like my nonna. I like the physical act of it—it's kind of a workout—and it doesn't take that much longer than using a machine. Though it does take a bit more practice to get it right, it's totally worth the extra effort. To make tonnarelli—long squared-sided strands and Rome's signature fresh pasta shape—you'll need a tool called a chitarra, which is sold for around $40 online. Make ridges on potato gnocchi with a dedicated tool called a gnocchi board, or use the tines of a fork to do the same job. Finally, a ruler will help you measure the thickness of your pasta strands, whether they are long, thin tagliatelle, small square pieces for tortellini, or rectangular sheets for cannelloni.

Ladle

Many dishes in this book use a ladleful of pasta cooking water, which is added to the sauce to thicken it and help it bind to the pasta. A ladleful is equivalent to ½ cup. If you don't have a ladle, you can use a ½-cup measuring cup or a mug with similar volume instead to transfer pasta cooking water to the pan. My ladle, a pewter antique from Italy, is so essential to my cooking that he even has a name: Bruno. I also use him along with a large serving fork I call Antoinetta to swirl pasta into neat nests when I plate it. Don't rule out giving an Italian name to your own ladle and twirling fork!

Olive Oil Cruet

I recommend a cruet for pouring extra-virgin olive oil, both because it can be a gorgeous design piece for your kitchen but also because it helps you pour olive oil without drips or spills.

Pepper Mill

Use a pepper mill for freshly grinding black peppercorns. If you buy pepper pre-ground, the aromas and deep essence will have already been lost, as pepper loses its flavor and goes stale quite quickly once it has been ground. Grinding it fresh releases the aroma and flavor exactly when you need it.

Potato Ricer

You will need to rice potatoes to get the right consistency for Homemade Potato Gnocchi (page 18). A potato ricer pushes the potatoes through small holes with a force that makes them smooth enough for the gnocchi. You won't get the same results with a box grater, food mill, or food processor, so if you plan to make potato gnocchi, a ricer is a must.

Pots and Pans

If you can, invest in very good pots and pans. I love cooking with copper, which lasts a lifetime and, in my opinion, is unbeatable for performance. It distributes heat evenly and produces amazing results. Copper, of course, is an investment. You can cook in just about anything, including warped pans rife with hot spots—as I used to in my very first kitchen—as long as your dish is seasoned with love and passion. But investing in good cookware will make cooking pasta, and everything else, even more gorgeous.

POTS: I use 8- to 12-quart pots to boil water for cooking pasta. Unless otherwise noted, you should fill the pot nearly to the top, leaving 2 inches unfilled. If you have a lid, too, that's great. Although it's not necessary, the water will boil faster if it's covered.

PANS: The recipes in this book were developed with a high-sided stainless-steel sauté pan (12-inch diameter and about 4 inches deep), a well-seasoned 12-inch cast-iron skillet, and a 14-inch copper skillet, all made from heavy-duty materials, which produce a more stable temperature while cooking. Still, you can use any pans you have, as long as they are large and deep enough to accommodate the sauces and the pasta comfortably. After you've cooked the pasta most of the way in boiling water, you will usually finish it in the pan with the sauce and some pasta water, and it will cook more evenly if you use a larger pan so the pasta has space to mingle. Deep pans also make tossing and swirling the pasta with the sauce easier—and less messy!

Sieves

I almost never drain pasta—shells for stuffing and pasta for cold salads are among the few exceptions. I need the tears of the gods, the precious cooking water and its

starchy luxury, to complete most recipes. Usually I use a spider strainer or tongs to transfer the pasta to the awaiting sauce. While cooking, you can also use a colander that nests in your pot so when you pull it out, it leaves most of the cooking water behind. If you must drain your pasta, be sure to keep plenty of pasta cooking water set aside, especially if the recipe calls for very al dente (see my definition, page xxii) pasta, since you will be cooking it for several minutes in the sauce and will need lots of extra liquid in the form of pasta cooking water to do that without drying everything out.

Wooden Spoons

I like massaging the pasta into its sauce for the ultimate mantecatura (see Mantecare, page xxii) with a set of wooden spoons. I think a sauce tastes better when it's mixed with wood instead of metal, which I feel reacts differently with the pasta.

INGREDIENTS *(hair flip)*

Friends always ask me how I can cook something so delicious with just a few simple ingredients. The answer is in the question itself: the ingredients. I cook with fresh, seasonal produce, the highest-quality extra-virgin olive oil I can find, and expertly made pasta for just gorgeous results. I always have. I grew up cooking with my grandmother near Naples, often with ingredients harvested just a few steps from the house, their ripened aromas permeating the kitchen. At home in Rome, we shopped at the market daily for fresh produce, meat, and fish. Whether harvesting them myself or selecting them from a market stall, I know that local fruits, vegetables, and herbs in season just taste better. For proof, tear a basil leaf that has been plucked directly from a thriving plant in season and compare it to picked basil from the supermarket. The aromas of the fresh basil will overwhelm you with their beauty.

When I moved to the US, I was worried that I wouldn't be able to match the quality of the ingredients I used in Italy. And honestly, there are some major differences. But there is also an incredible network of small farms across America that are just as dedicated to the land as Nonno Agostino was. In the beginning, I spent a lot of time vetting farms and sourcing produce because I wanted to know where my food came from, who grew it, and how it was grown. In the process, I discovered some incredible local farms like Full Circle Farm in Live Oak, Florida. Some participate in farmers' markets or offer CSA boxes, while others fly under the radar because, well, they are busy farming.

With a little curiosity, patience, and effort, I know you can find just gorgeous ingredients near you, too, whether by finding a farm yourself or frequenting your local farmers' market on a regular basis. I promise you that one of the most beautiful things in life is building relationships with the people who make and grow your ingredients. Your food will be so much better for it, and you'll be supporting local agriculture and helping it to thrive in the process.

For recipes listed by season, like summer's Ziti alla Norma (page 97) and fall's Fusillata Casareccia ai Funghi (page 91), visit the pasta index on page 239. Other recipes feature pantry items that are available year-round. The list in Resources (page 237) includes my favorite online vendors for canned tomatoes, salted anchovies, and other Italian pantry staples. Building an Italian pantry doesn't happen overnight, but the process of filling your cupboards with beautiful ingredients is a gorgeous labor of love.

Anchovies

I use salt-packed anchovies, which have a much more mellow flavor than the oil-packed variety, which honestly are so often rancid they have turned generations of pasta lovers against anchovies in general. I love salted anchovies from Cetara on the Amalfi Coast or from Sciacca in southwestern Sicily and buy them from Italian specialty stores and online. If you prefer oil-packed anchovies, be sure to get them from a reputable source that protects the fish and their oil from temperature fluctuations during transit, which contributes to rancidity.

Black Pepper

Once an exotic spice that few could afford, black pepper is now one of the most common kitchen staples. I always use freshly ground black pepper from my pepper mill, which cracks each peppercorn coarsely, awakening its piquant aromas. I buy fresh peppercorns from a spice shop, which are often more potent than what you find at the grocery store.

Cheese

Italy is home to thousands of cheeses. Some are made by just a single farm, while others reach a global market. In my cooking, I use Pecorino Romano and Parmigiano-Reggiano most frequently, both of which are only made in Italy. You can, however, use domestic mozzarella with great results—in fact imported mozzarella has often lost its signature milky flavor by the time it lands in the US. Whatever your source, for maximum flavor use only freshly grated cheese and grate it to the fineness described in the recipe. This advice is so nice I'm telling my gorgeous friends twice: Never use pre-grated cheese. It is too dry, it is rarely fresh, and it is often packed with additives. Now buckle up for a crash course in my favorite cheeses to cook with and how to use them!

PECORINO ROMANO: This salted, aged sheep's milk cheese is a cornerstone of Roman cooking and it is added to recipes like Rigatoni alla Gricia (page 46) and emulsified to form a creamy sauce. In other cases, it is grated and dusted over plated pasta. The flavor is deep and salt-forward, and its intense, savory notes make it a protagonist in many dishes, rather than a supporting character.

If a sauce calls for Pecorino Romano, I base the fineness of the grate on how I intend to use it. For melting the cheese into a sauce, I love a very fine grate from the smallest punched holes of a box grater, while a Microplane grate offers a nice flurry of cheese that can fall into nooks and crannies when grated directly over a dish. For my recipes, a younger pecorino, aged around nine months, will melt more consistently than a more aged one, which by nature is drier.

As its name implies, Pecorino Romano has Roman origins: During the empire, soldiers would eat aged pecorino that was similar to the modern version to give them energy. Over the centuries, the tradition of sheep's milk cheese remained strong in Rome, where there was a great appetite for it. Eventually, the demand for the cheese spread all over the world, but Pecorino Romano, by law, is made in just three Italian regions: Lazio, Tuscany, and Sardinia. There are no true domestic substitutes for Pecorino Romano.

PARMIGIANO-REGGIANO: Like Pecorino Romano, Parmigiano-Reggiano is a legally defined style of cheese making. In order to bear its prestigious name, the cheese must be made with cow's milk in a limited area in northern Italy near Parma. The cheese is aged for a minimum of 12 months, and the longer it ages, the more complex and concentrated the flavors and aromas become. I save a 36-month aged Parmigiano-Reggiano for eating on its own, and cook with a younger 12- to 18-month Parmigiano-Reggiano. I never throw away a Parmigiano rind of any age. I keep them to add to broths like brodo di cappone (see page 145) and pasta minestrata recipes like The Lazy Princess (page 210) to enrich their flavor.

Parmigiano-Reggiano definitely has a nuttier, milder, and more nuanced flavor profile than Pecorino Romano, which makes it a wonderful supporting character to enhance a dish's ingredients without overwhelming them. It is a staple in dishes with creamy pasta sauces such as Tortellini alla Panna (page 131) and baked pastas like Radiatori al Forno (page 166).

Although it is originally from the north of Italy, Parmigiano-Reggiano has been fully adopted across the country's twenty regions. It is used in thousands of dishes, although it is rarely, if ever, combined with seafood.

MOZZARELLA: Mozzarella is deeply rooted in the Italian south, especially Campania, and you must make it a priority to taste it there at least once in your life (it may ruin all future mozzarella for you, but it's totally worth it). I grew up eating fresh mozzarella that was less than 24 hours old and had been stretched by hand over massive steaming vats—I literally snacked on that instead of cookies—and I still believe that's the best way to consume it. There's nothing like slicing into a mozzarella ball that "cries" milky tears of freshness and devouring it on the spot.

I recommend finding a local source that produces fresh mozzarella rather than using an imported variety. By the time it arrives from Italy, the mozzarella is many days past its prime. With every hour that passes from its production, the mozzarella's flavor and structure change, eventually taking on a tangy acidity and dry texture that are sacrilege.

Artisanal mozzarella making starts with cow's milk, which is pasteurized and combined with whey from the previous day's cheesemaking. The mixture is heated

and fermented, and then the curds are stretched and pulled into balls, braids, or knots. An expert mozzarella maker knows not only how to shape the cheese but also how to squeeze out the right amount of liquid to make it springy and juicy while not overly wet. Look for the freshest mozzarella you can find and always drain it before cooking—otherwise, the liquid it releases can make your dish very soggy.

PROVOLONE: This cow's milk cheese is quite similar to mozzarella. Its curds are also stretched and formed after fermentation, but more moisture is squeezed out of them to create a more solid, compact, and dry texture than fresh mozzarella. Provolone melts beautifully, and I love draping slices over my Cannelloni (page 184), coarsely shredding it into Pasta con le Patate (page 77), or draping over Finger Food Pasta Bake (page 168) to add a gooey depth. Provolone comes in several forms. I love the piquant Provolone del Monaco, imported from the Amalfi Coast. If you can't find it, look for a different strongly flavored provolone instead.

RICOTTA: Ricotta is made from the whey left behind after cow, sheep, goat, or buffalo cheese is made. Ricotta isn't actually cheese, but rather a dairy by-product. The whey is combined with an acid component and reheated (*ricotta* means "cooked again" in Italian), and the soft curds that emerge from this mixture are drained and packaged for sale. Fresh ricotta, if you're lucky enough to find it, has the sweet flavor of fresh milk. Its texture differs from brand to brand, and I always taste my ricotta before cooking with it. If it is watery, I line a colander with cheesecloth, pour the ricotta into it, and drain until it loses some of its moisture. If the ricotta is very granular, I will buzz it in a food processor until it is smooth. Homemade ricotta is easy to make; see my instructions on page 186.

I personally love sheep's milk ricotta, and it's the most common in Rome, produced after Pecorino Romano or another sheep's milk cheese is made. Use it if you can find it, to enjoy the extra richness it has compared to other types. If cow's milk ricotta is all you can find, be sure to season it with salt, as it is typically very delicate or even bland on its own. Mix any quality ricotta into dishes like Lemon Ricotta Delight (page 229) for gorgeous flavor and to enhance the creaminess of a sauce.

RICOTTA SALATA: *Ricotta salata* means "salted ricotta," and it is just that. Ricotta is massaged with salt and its flavor intensifies and moisture reduces, making it compact and grateable. It's a common ingredient in Sicily and appears in a flurry on top of Ziti alla Norma (page 97). No need to season ricotta salata.

Chili Peppers

Most Italians avoid spicy peppers, but in the south of Italy, especially in Campania and Calabria, we love a bit of heat. I use fresh cayenne and Calabrian chilies that I grow in my garden, or Calabrian chili paste that I buy online. You can use whatever kind of spicy chili pepper you prefer. Generally, the recipes call for fresh chili peppers, but you can also use dried; several also list dried chili flakes. When it comes to chili flakes, it's key that they're fresh so they pack a punch; if kept in a well-sealed container they will stay fresh for up to 6 months. To determine whether they are fresh or stale, just taste them. If you really want to channel your inner Southern Italian, serve pasta beside whole chilies with a knife or scissors, so you and your guests can add the exact amount of heat you want.

Cured Meats

For thousands of years, Italians have been curing meat, especially pork, to extend its shelf life. The methods used today are similar to those from Roman times: whole muscles like haunch (prosciutto), jowl (guanciale), and belly (pancetta) are massaged with salt and spices, then allowed to age in cool, ventilated places until they reach the ideal flavor and texture. In Italy, each *alimentari* (small grocery or deli) and supermarket stocks a range of guanciale and pancetta, and the butcher will slice them into slabs, strips, or cubes based on what you are cooking and your preferences. Although guanciale is still a cornerstone of Rome's pasta classics, like Carbonara (page 39), Amatriciana (page 43), and Gricia (page 46), some Romans prefer pancetta. While quite similar in their application, guanciale is much fattier than pancetta and has a more savory flavor.

PROSCIUTTO: Prosciutto, the back haunches of a pig, can be *crudo* ("raw" is the literal translation, but in practice it means cured) or *cotto* ("cooked"; similar to American deli ham). All across Italy, prosciutto crudo is sliced into beautiful pink ribbons and arranged on charcuterie boards. It can be sliced or torn into small pieces and added to recipes like Rigatoni alla Papalina (page 66) to deliver its savory flavor and tender texture. In my recipes, I refer to the cured version as prosciutto. When I use cotto in recipes, such as in Tortellini alla Panna (page 131), I refer to it as ham.

GUANCIALE: Cured pork jowl is a fundamental Roman ingredient and appears in the city's most famous dishes, like Carbonara (page 39), Amatriciana (page 43), and Gricia (page 46). It is cut into slabs like bacon, then cut crosswise to make tiles for cooking. Its flavor is strong and a bit gamey, and it produces quite a bit of fat when rendered. It can be a little hard to find in the US and doesn't have the same freshness or fat content as it does in Italy. If I can find a really good source, I'll use it. Otherwise I will substitute with good pancetta, which is easier to find here.

PANCETTA: Pancetta is cured pork belly that has been salted and aged. It may also be smoked, but I prefer the unsmoked variety. It is the cousin to bacon, which is salted and smoked pork belly. When you slice pancetta open, you will recognize the layers of white fat and the pink meat of bacon. In spite of their similarities, Italians reach for pancetta over bacon. It is cut into strips and heated in a pan to render its fat, which gives flavor to sauces. Its flavor is sweeter and milder than that of guanciale, and it has about 30 percent less fat.

Dried Pasta

Dried pasta is produced all over Italy, but my favorite brands are from my ancestral homeland of Campania. Always use high-quality dried pasta made from a durum wheat dough that has been extruded through a textured bronze die (never smooth plastic or a non-stick coated material) and dried very slowly to preserve its integrity. You can tell the difference by touching the pasta's surface: Bronze-extruded pasta will have a rough texture, while nonstick-extruded pasta will feel smooth to the touch. Italian brands will also feature the phrase *trafilata al bronzo* ("bronze-extruded") on their packaging if they use bronze dies. Any of the pasta recipes in the book can be made with gluten-free pasta. You can find my favorite brands, including gluten-free ones, in Resources (page 237).

Eggs

My recipes use large eggs. Use the most natural and organic ones you can find. I get eggs from a local farm and if you can, I suggest you do, too.

Extra-Virgin Olive Oil

Olive oil is one of the most essential ingredients in my cooking. I use extra-virgin cold-pressed oil, which is made with underripe olives grown and harvested by hand in Italy. You should be able to sense how fresh your oil is by smelling and tasting it. Fresh oil tastes like the juices of pressed olives, and it should burn the back of your throat thanks to the antioxidants it contains. Unlike wine, olive oil is best consumed fresh—be suspicious of any place that tries to peddle oil that is more than a year and a half old. Unfortunately a lot of olive oil found on supermarket shelves and even in home kitchens is far from fresh and is in fact rancid—it tastes bad and smells of wet cardboard.

Be sure to keep your oil in a dark, well-sealed container to protect it from light and oxidation. Keep it away from heat, which includes your stovetop. And, if possible, invest in a good olive oil that comes from a trackable source. Many olive oils are made with fruit from anonymous sources or fruit that has been harvested past its prime or damaged. Quality olive oil is always worth the investment. It will take your dish to the next level.

Flour

Most of the recipes in this book call for dried pasta, which is made from a durum wheat and water dough extruded through a machine that cuts it into a specific shape.

Durum wheat grows mainly in Southern Italy, and durum wheat flour is sold in two forms: a coarse flour called semolina, and a finer version called *farina di semola rimacinata*, which is closer in texture to all-purpose flour. I use coarse semolina when I want to give texture to pasta, as in Pasta Acqua e Farina (page 30), and I use a bit of it alongside soft wheat in Tonnarelli (page 14), to give them a bit more bite and firm texture.

The other fresh pasta recipes call for all-purpose flour or 00 flour, both of which are typically made from soft wheat. All-purpose flour, as the name implies, is good for virtually any basic kitchen use. Its high protein level (and, therefore, high amount of gluten) is suitable for fresh pasta, which needs gluten to hold its shape. "Tipo 00" flour is a refined white flour that has been finely milled. The number refers to the milling fineness, not a particular use, so be sure to get 00 flour specifically made for pasta. This should be noted on the packaging. I prefer Italian brands for my own cooking, but if you're using domestic flour, choose organic if you can.

Garlic

Always use fresh cloves, never dried garlic powder. Ever. Promise me. At times, garlic is left whole; most of the time it is minced (chopped as finely as possible). It should always be peeled.

Throughout the recipes, I instruct you to cook garlic in oil for just a few minutes, which guarantees that beautiful flavors will permeate your dish. When garlic turns brown or burns, the flavor becomes unpleasant and bitter, so take care to cook it gently until it turns blond—the only time that I prefer blonds to brunettes! Whether you leave it in the sauce or take it out after this step is up to you. I do either, depending on my mood. Leaving it in will infuse the dish with a deeper garlic flavor, while taking it out will create a more subtle effect. Various gradients of aroma are released based on how the garlic is prepared. You can cook it whole and it will release just a light aroma. The aroma intensifies in this order: used whole without peel, sliced, finely minced.

Herbs

I only use fresh herbs, and I have my own garden for a steady supply. I love tending to my basil, parsley, mint, sage, rosemary, and thyme. I cannot live without them in my recipes, and I nurture them like my own children. Picking fresh herbs gives food unbelievable flavor and, with a bit of windowsill space, you can grow your own, too. If you haven't already tried this, I cannot tell you how gratifying it is. If you don't grow your own, if possible purchase potted herbs for their superior flavor and avoid precut, packaged herbs if you can. I avoid dried herbs altogether. I find they tend to have a bitter flavor and don't taste anything like their fresh counterparts.

When a recipe calls for herbs, I will give the quantity in the ingredients list, but I leave it up to you and your tastes to determine how much basil, parsley, oregano, or other fresh herbs you'd like to use as a garnish. I will also specify whether you will need whole leaves, roughly chopped (a few good whacks to a pile with a sharp knife will do), finely chopped (think a really fine confetti), or torn. I always tear basil to release its beautiful aromas and never cut it with a knife, which bruises the delicate leaf.

Rice

In Southern Italy there isn't a lot of risotto, or other rice dishes, which are more common in Northern Italy. But I absolutely love risotto, which is why I put it in my pasta book. It's also a gluten-free alternative to wheat-based pastas. One of my favorite things about risotto—and I hope it will become yours, too—is the gentle care it requires as it cooks. Rice (I like the Carnaroli and Arborio varieties) is first toasted in oil and aromatics, and then bathed with small amounts of liquid until it is cooked through. The creaminess of this labor of love is enhanced with the mantecatura, mixing in butter, cheese, or olive oil passionately at the end for a luscious finish.

Salt

Like pepper, salt was once a precious ingredient used to preserve foods. It was even used to pay soldiers in ancient times, giving us the word "salary." Now it is affordable and used for seasoning, too. Romans in particular have a pretty heavy hand when

it comes to salting foods. I like to salt throughout the cooking process, layering in flavor as I go and leveraging all of its seasoning potential. I rain a shower of salt onto diced onions or shallots as they are sizzling in oil to help release their inner essence. I season tomatoes, meats, and vegetables when I add them to the pan and always taste a dish before serving it, adjusting the seasoning before it goes to the table. Not all salts pack the same amount of flavor, so I don't give salt quantities in the ingredients lists. Use your senses to season your food.

I only use unrefined sea salt, which is not treated with any additives or caking agents. It is the most natural salt ingredient, harvested in pools near the sea, which makes me feel connected to my Italian roots. Right now, I am using a lot of *sel gris* (gray salt), which is hand-harvested and sun-dried on France's Atlantic coast, and that brings a beautiful minerality to the ingredients.

Tomatoes

This ingredient, perhaps more than any other, is the most iconic Italian ingredient after pasta itself. Tomatoes originally came from Mesoamerica and only arrived in Europe in the mid-sixteenth century, and it wasn't until three hundred years later, in the nineteenth century, that they were adopted into Italian cooking, specifically in the south. Now it's impossible to imagine Italian cuisine without them. Today there are many kinds of tomatoes, sometimes named for where they grow. Pomodoro del Piennolo del Vesuvio calls out the volcano on and around which it grows, while Pomodoro di Pachino refers to a number of tomatoes that grow around the Sicilian village of Pachino. San Marzano is a plum variety with a thick skin that grows near Naples.

My recipes call for tomatoes in a number of forms: fresh tomatoes in season, canned whole peeled tomatoes, and occasionally tomato puree. I have a strong preference for canned whole peeled tomatoes. I typically only use crushed tomatoes if I am very sure they come from a quality source. I never use tomato sauce that is already flavored or sweetened. Fresh tomatoes and canned whole peeled tomatoes should have a balance of sweetness, acidity, and savoriness. I only use tomato puree when I know the source.

I also use tomato paste in some recipes. The process to make this is incredible. Tomatoes are picked at their peak of ripeness, then cooked down. The cooked sauce is drained of its liquid, leaving the powerfully flavorful tomato pulp behind. It is then spread out to dry in the sun, which intensifies its flavor. Hundreds of tomatoes are required to make a single can. So imagine the power of pure tomato essence that you get in every spoonful.

I use fresh tomatoes when they are in season, while I use high-quality canned tomatoes year-round, since they are typically picked at their height of ripeness. Taste your canned tomatoes before you cook with them. An excellent canned tomato can take me back to my family's annual summer harvest with my grandparents, when everyone would get together and jar tomatoes for the coming year. We always picked the ripest fruit and never had to add sugar afterward to balance their flavor. If you have to add sugar to your canned tomatoes, it's time to break up with your brand.

Wine and Spirits

Alcohol transmits flavor and helps a dish's ingredients melt into one another. To be clear, I'm not seeking to use alcohol itself. When I add wine, vodka, or whiskey to my dishes, the alcohol content evaporates almost entirely. What's left behind are the nuances of the beverage, so you get those amazing flavors without the alcohol. I always cook with very good-quality wine—something you would actually want to pour for yourself and your guests to drink. In fact, if I use wine in a recipe, I serve the rest of the bottle with the meal! I use any good-quality vodka and whiskey that I would enjoy in a cocktail.

The ART *of* ENTERTAINING

Food and entertainment have been the key to celebrating, forming alliances, and creating unbreakable bonds of love and friendship for thousands of years. You can take part in this ancient, sacred ritual in your own kitchen. Entertaining should start with yourself. So don't host a party or even cook for your family if you aren't in a good mood. If I am feeling out of sorts, I will take a barefoot walk on the beach or do a little bit of gardening and take care of my herbs to snap me out of it. Everyone has their own ways of soothing—pour yourself a glass of wine, meditate, or do whatever sets you right! The way you feel transfers to the plate, so if you cook while stressed, I guarantee your guests will feel and taste that. I also deeply believe that cooking while looking and feeling gorgeous translates to better pasta dishes. Dressing up and loving yourself, letting yourself revel in your gorgeousness, is my first secret to a successful meal. Once you're in the state of mind for cooking an amazing meal, here are some other things you can do to make your pasta perfection rise to even greater heights.

Set the Mood
Put on some music and light some candles. Build your tablescape. You start digesting with your eyes before you even take a bite of food, so setting the table and adorning it thoughtfully goes a long way to telling your guests that mealtime is special, no matter the occasion. I love decorating the table with ingredients from the recipe—bundles of basil and rosemary or lemons and lemon leaves—which really connects everyone to what's on their plate. Fresh plants and flowers are a beautiful addition, too. I use anything that brings a sense of nature and freshness to the room. Use what you have to make your table look just as gorgeous as the pasta that awaits.

Pick Your Plate
Some pasta dishes are best served on a platter for family-style dining. Sharing is such a beautiful way to enjoy pasta together. Invest in one special platter that you use for presenting your pasta. It should feel good to hold and tell everyone who sees it that you care about the details.

(Almost) Always Garnish
Nearly every pasta recipe I make is served with a garnish—the exceptions are a few of the baked pasta dishes. Sometimes my garnishes are playful, like whole chilies, while other times they are herbs like basil or parsley that enhance the aromatics of a recipe. No matter how small or seemingly insignificant, taking that extra moment to embellish a dish makes it even more special.

Build Beautiful Nests

My ladle, Bruno, is probably my most precious kitchen tool. Not only does he deliver the tears of the gods in a steady stream to my sauces, but he also conspires with my *forchetta*, a large serving fork called Antonietta, to create the perfect mountain of pasta. She is the strength behind Bruno, and tames long pasta strands into beautiful nests as she twirls in Bruno's deep bowl. Once Antonietta has done her work, you can shimmy the pasta nest you've created onto a plate to create something just gorgeous.

———

With these tips in mind, think about what your unique hospitality style could be, and then kick it into action the next time you cook!

CHAPTER ONE

PASTA
BASICS

A BRIEF HISTORY *of* PASTA

When I was growing up, I always heard the myth that the Italian explorer Marco Polo introduced pasta to Venice in the thirteenth century after encountering it in China. Like many myths, it does hold a kernel of truth: Polo certainly encountered food in the Far East that would be considered pasta today. But he was almost definitely already a pasta eater when he set sail from his home in Venice. I like to imagine it was the last meal his wife served him before he departed, and what inspired him to find his way home!

Pasta has been made in Italy for thousands of years, even before Roman times. The Greeks brought it from its original home in the Far East, where traces of pasta stretch back more than ten thousand years. While Italians didn't invent pasta, I like to think we perfected it. Dried pasta was introduced to the south of Italy in the form of couscous and *itriya* (strands) by Arab settlers in the ninth century—a pretty important cultural moment when eggplants, spices, sugar, and citrus also arrived. Drying pasta made it portable and easy to take on long voyages, as fleets sought to build and expand empires. It literally fueled some of the most advanced conquests in Europe's history, but it didn't take off in Italy until nearly a thousand years later!

By the Renaissance, cookbooks published in Italy for nobles featured pasta recipes including spices like cinnamon and nutmeg and sweeteners like sugar, a reminder that pasta is a diverse food that doesn't have to follow all the rules we give it today. While popes and kings were feasting on elaborate and intensely flavored casseroles made from fresh pasta, pasta remained a luxury for most who only ate it on holidays. As Italy industrialized and became a unified nation in the late nineteenth century, certain foods went from niche regional specialties to national dishes. Dried pasta made near Naples and Gragnano was one of them, and it eventually reached every corner of the Italian map. In the twentieth century, as modern Italian cuisine was born and developed, dried pasta was at its center. Everyone could afford it, and it didn't require the precious resources of time and ingredients that fresh pasta demanded. Soon, in a country in which pasta had originally been a luxury, it came to embody the very essence of being Italian.

Dried vs Fresh Pasta

In Italy, pasta is a massive category of food, but we can generally divide it into two types: dried and fresh. Both are essentially made in the same way. Flour is mixed with liquid such as water or eggs, which hydrates the flour and activates the gluten network. The gluten is further developed—and strengthened—by kneading. Then, the dough is shaped and boiled. The type of flour you use, and how it is worked, will determine the pasta's shape and texture.

DRIED PASTA MADE FROM DURUM FLOUR: Dried pasta is made from durum wheat flour and water. Durum wheat is a type of wheat that grows very well in Southern Italy. When milled, it makes a grainy flour called semolina or a powdery flour called *farina di semola rimacinata.*

The rougher surface of "bronze-extruded" pasta creates a bigger surface area for releasing starch into the water as the pasta boils, which is ideal for making silky sauces with the tears of the gods. Plus a rough texture also attracts sauce, making it adhere perfectly. Companies that use a bronze die also dry their pasta much more slowly than the massive industrial pasta brands, mimicking the old custom of drying pasta in the sun, and I like that connection to tradition.

Most of the recipes in this book called for dried pasta shapes, including the world-renowned spaghetti and linguine, but there are also lesser-known shapes like lumache and ditalini. The world of pasta shapes is vast, and I hope you enjoy discovering new (to you) shapes throughout your pasta journey!

FRESH PASTA MADE FROM SOFT WHEAT FLOUR: Fresh pasta may be made with durum wheat (as in the case of Pasta Acqua e Farina, page 30, for orecchiette) or potatoes (for Homemade Potato Gnocchi, page 18), but most of the fresh pasta in this book, and in Italy in general, is *pasta all'uovo* made with soft wheat and egg (see Sfoglia all'Uovo, page 9). Some make *pasta all'uovo* with whole eggs, while others uses only yolks; the choice is largely determined by how your nonna made pasta. Whole eggs marry the protein from the egg white, which contributes structure, with the fat from the yolk, which makes the dough more pliable. Yolk-only dough tends to be a bit glossier due to the fat. Making dough with yolks only generates a whole lot of egg white waste (and let's face it, even with the best intentions I rarely make meringues from the egg whites I set aside after fresh pasta making), so I recommend using the whole egg. I do add a little bit of semolina to the soft wheat flour for my Tonnarelli dough (page 14) to add a little more strength and bite.

Within the category, there are pasta sheets for lasagna and cannelloni as well as long strands like tagliolini, fettuccine, tagliatelle, and pappardelle. There is also *pasta ripiena* ("filled pasta") like tortellini and ravioli.

FRESH PASTA MADE FROM DURUM WHEAT FLOUR: In the south of Italy, we often combine durum wheat and water to make small, hand-shaped pastas like orecchiette (see Pasta Acqua e Farina, page 30). The characteristics of durum wheat flour make it ideal for stubby shapes. When you mix durum wheat with water and knead it, you create a strong dough that feels tough under your fingertips. The water hydrates the flour, and that activates the flour's main proteins to form gluten. Gluten's proteins bring their own characteristics to the mix and together they form the gluten network. Some proteins promote extensibility. Others allow a dough to become elastic, meaning the dough will spring back to its original shape when stretched. Durum wheat is rich in elastic protein, so when you try to roll it into sheets, it snaps back like a rubber band. This means durum wheat is not ideal for long, snappy noodles, but it's great for short, irregular hand-shaped pasta.

My Fresh Pasta Dough Recipes

I love dried pasta and am obsessed with its gorgeous flavor and structure. But in my family, some fresh pasta shapes are made for special occasions as a way to show extra love. They include golden and green sheets of *sfoglia all'uovo*, plump potato gnocchi, beautifully shaped tortellini, delicate ravioli, classic Roman tonnarelli, and Pasta Acqua e Farina (page 30) for making orecchiette. Each recipe includes metric units, which are far more accurate than volume when measuring flour, so I suggest you use a scale until you master each recipe and can measure and mix by feel just like an Italian nonna.

RULES *for* MAKING PERFECT PASTA THE PASTA QUEEN WAY

These rules and techniques are the pillars of my pasta-making secrets, and they are foolproof ways to take your pasta to royal heights.

1. I add salt to the water once it's reached a rolling boil, and before dropping my pasta in. Adding salt lowers the boiling point of the water and I want it the hottest it can be when I drop the pasta in. I want the salt to season the pasta, so always add it abundantly until the water tastes like a seasoned soup.

2. Treat the recommended cooking time on a box of dried pasta as a guide, not law, to tell you when the pasta is al dente. Use your senses and taste the pasta as it cooks to achieve your perfect bite!

3. I always aim for very al dente or al dente pasta, depending on whether I finish the pasta in the sauce for a few minutes or just stir vigorously to dress it. Overcooking is the death of pasta and makes it soft and tragic. Don't worry: I'll always tell you to what degree the pasta should be cooked.

4. I never drain pasta cooking water before I plate and serve pasta. Using it makes your sauce creamier at the end, and keeping it hot and boiling helps you finish sauces faster. Depending on the pasta shape, use a spider strainer, a slotted spoon, or tongs to transfer your pasta from the pot of water to the sauce pan so you have plenty of hot pasta cooking water bubbling away and ready to use as you finish your dish.

5. When the recipe calls for very al dente pasta, transfer it to the sauce with some pasta cooking water, adding more as needed to finish cooking the pasta without letting the sauce get too dry.

6. Stir with the passion of an Italian. Many pasta sauces rely on mantecatura (see Mantecare, page xxii) for their creamy texture. To use pasta water to your advantage, harness the starch of the tears of the gods, and stir your pasta enthusiastically and with love using two wooden spoons until it is silky and smooth. If you have the right pans you can *saltare la pasta* (sort of flip the pasta in the pan). This vigorous tossing in the pan helps to bind the pasta and sauce together for the perfect mantecatura.

SFOGLIA *all'*UOVO

FRESH EGG PASTA DOUGH
FOR LASAGNA, CANNELLONI,
TAGLIOLINI, FETTUCCINE,
TAGLIATELLE, AND
PAPPARDELLE

Makes about 1 pound
(4 servings)

Total prep and cooking time:
1 hour 15 minutes

300 grams (about 1¾ cups
plus 2 tablespoons) all-purpose
or 00 flour

3 large eggs, at room temperature

The *sfoglia*, a sheet of pasta made from an egg-enriched dough, is incredibly versatile. It can be rolled with a pasta machine (see Pasta Machine Instructions, page 10) or rolling pin (see Rolling Pasta by Hand, page 12). It can be cut into large pieces to make layers for Lasagna al Ragù di Lady Caterina (page 71) or rectangles to make ricotta-filled Cannelloni (page 184) tubes. It can also be rolled and sliced into thin or thick strips to make golden strands of tagliolini, fettuccine, tagliatelle, and pappardelle. My family uses whole eggs for their sfoglia, which gives the cooked pasta a gorgeous texture that has a little more bite to it than yolk-only dough, thanks to the protein from the egg white. Use the best and most natural eggs you can find for this recipe, and then follow the instructions below to make the shape you desire.

Pour the flour onto your work surface and use your fingers or a spoon to make a well in the center. Crack the eggs into the well and gently beat them together with a fork. Little by little, working from the inside of the well to the edges, bring some flour into the egg mixture, stirring with a fork until each portion of flour is incorporated. When the egg mixture is no longer runny, begin kneading the dough with your hands, feeling how it changes beneath your fingertips as you work.

Use your whole body to rock back and forth over the dough, pressing it against your work surface and away from you until the eggs and flour have become one. Continue kneading to strengthen the dough, working it over like a lover, until it is strong and glossy and springs back when you press a finger into it. Wrap tightly with plastic wrap and refrigerate for 30 minutes.

Unwrap the pasta dough.

recipe continues

Pasta Machine Instructions

Cut the dough into 4 equal pieces and flatten each to a uniform thickness. Run each dough piece through a pasta machine, starting on the widest setting and repeating on successively thinner settings until it is almost transparent. Pasta machines typically make long sheets 6 inches wide.

For lasagna: Cut the pasta sheet into pieces that fit your baking dish. Assemble the lasagna according to the instructions on page 71. You do not need to cook the pasta in advance; it will cook as it bakes.

For cannelloni: Cut the pasta sheet into 6 × 8-inch rectangles. Assemble the cannelloni according to the recipe on page 185. You do not need to cook the pasta in advance; it will cook as it bakes.

For tagliolini: Cut the sheet into 12-inch-long pieces. Use the 3-millimeter (0.12-inch) setting to cut the pasta into thin strands. Unfurl the strands, fashion them into a nest, and set aside until you are ready to cook them in salted boiling water, 30 seconds to 1 minute.

For fettuccine: Cut the sheet into 12-inch-long pieces. Use the 5-millimeter (0.2-inch) setting to cut the pasta into thin strands. Unfurl the strands, fashion them into a nest, and set aside until you are ready to cook them in salted boiling water, 1 to 2 minutes.

For tagliatelle: Cut the sheet into 12-inch-long pieces. Use the 7-millimeter (0.3-inch) setting to cut the pasta into thin strands. Unfurl the strands, fashion them into a nest, and set aside until you are ready to cook them in salted boiling water, 1 to 2 minutes.

For pappardelle: Cut the sheet into 12-inch long pieces. Use the 19-millimeter (¾-inch) setting to cut the pasta into thin strands. Unfurl the strands, fashion them into a nest, and set aside until you are ready to cook them in salted boiling water, 1 to 2 minutes.

recipe continues

Rolling Pasta by Hand

Rolling your own pasta is rewarding on so many levels, and a bonus is having leftover scraps of dough that are *maltagliati*, Italian for "badly cut." These irregular pasta scraps are brilliant for using in brothy sauces and soups like Pasta e Fagioli (page 60) or Pastina in Brodo (page 138), and are a reminder that, just like my nonna taught me, it's a sin to waste anything. Maltagliati will keep well wrapped in the freezer for up to 4 months.

Lightly dust a work surface with flour. Position the dough on the floured surface and press it into a disk of uniform thickness. Dust the surface of the dough with flour. Place your rolling pin in the middle of the disk. Working from the middle outward, push the rolling pin over the dough with fluid movements, returning to the middle of the disk with each movement. Give the dough a quarter-turn and repeat until the dough is a nearly transparent round.

For lasagna: Cut the round into strips to create your pasta layers. Assemble the lasagna according the instructions on page 71.

For cannelloni: Cut the round into 5 × 8-inch pieces. Assemble the cannelloni according the recipe on page 185.

For tagliolini: Lightly dust the pasta round, then cut it in half. Position one semicircular piece of dough with the round end facing you. Beginning at one end, fold the piece into a loose tube. Square off each end and use the scraps for maltagliati. Use a sharp knife to cut the tube crosswise into strands 3 millimeters (0.12 inch) wide. Unfurl the strands, fashion them into a nest, and set aside until you are ready to cook them in salted boiling water, 30 seconds to 1 minute. Repeat with the other semicircle.

For fettuccine: Lightly dust the pasta round, then cut it in half. Position one semicircular piece of dough with the round end facing you. Beginning at one end, fold the piece into a loose tube. Square off each end and use the scraps for maltagliati. Use a sharp knife to cut each tube crosswise into strands 4 to 6 millimeters (0.15 to 0.25 inch) wide. Unfurl the strands, fashion them into a nest, and set aside until you are ready to cook them in salted boiling water, 1 to 2 minutes. Repeat with the other semicircle.

Maltagliati

Tagliolini

Fettuccine

Pappardelle

For tagliatelle: Lightly dust the pasta round, then cut it in half. Position one semicircular piece of dough with the round end facing you. Beginning at one end, fold the piece into a loose tube. Square off each end and use the scraps for maltagliati Use a sharp knife to cut each tube crosswise into strands 7 millimeters (0.3 inch) wide. Unfurl the strands, fashion them into a nest, and set aside until you are ready to cook them in salted boiling water, 1 to 2 minutes. Repeat with the other semicircle.

For pappardelle: Lightly dust the pasta round, then cut it in half. Position one semicircular piece of dough with the round end facing you. Beginning at one end, fold the piece into a loose tube. Square off each end and use the scraps for maltagliati. Use a sharp knife to cut each tube crosswise into strands 2 to 3 centimeters (0.75 to 1.15 inches) wide. Unfurl the strands, fashion them into a nest, and set aside until you are ready to cook them in salted boiling water, 1 to 2 minutes. Repeat with the other semicircle.

TONNARELLI

*Makes about 1 pound
(4 servings)*

———

*Total prep and cooking time:
1 hour*

250 grams (1½ cups plus
1 tablespoon) all-purpose or
00 flour, plus more for dusting

50 grams (about ¼ cup) semolina

195 grams (3 to 4 large) eggs,
at room temperature

GORGEOUS TIP

If you don't have a chitarra, you can cut the sheets into 12-inch-long strands with a sharp knife. Carefully measure the exact thickness of the pasta sheet (a metric ruler is the best for this), and then aim for cutting the strands that exact width.

Tonnarelli are the classic Roman pasta partner for cheesy Cacio e Pepe (page 36), and I am completely obsessed with their shape. While dried pasta has my heart, tonnarelli are my absolute favorite fresh pasta shape because they have such a satisfying texture and such a gorgeous bite to them. Think of tonnarelli as fresh spaghetti, but instead of the pasta strands being dried and round, they are long, square strands cut from golden sfoglia all'uovo with a bit of semolina added to them for a little extra bite. You may know them by their other name, spaghetti alla chitarra, which is a nod to the tool that is used to make them. The chitarra is a rectangular wooden instrument with wires pulled tightly across its surface. Once the pasta is rolled into sheets, the sheets are placed over these wires, dusted with flour, then rolled over with a rolling pin. The pasta strands are sliced by the wires, then fall into the compartment below to be collected for cooking.

Pour the all-purpose flour and semolina onto your work surface and use your fingers or a spoon to make a well in the center. Crack the eggs into the well and gently beat them together with a fork. Little by little and working from the inside of the well to the edges, bring some flour into the egg mixture, stirring with the fork until each portion of flour is incorporated. When the egg mixture is no longer runny, begin kneading the dough with your hands, feeling how it changes beneath your fingertips as you work.

Use your whole body to rock back and forth over the dough, pressing it against your work surface until the eggs and flour have become one. Continue kneading to strengthen the dough, working it over like a lover, until it is strong and glossy and it springs back when you press a finger into it. Wrap tightly with plastic wrap and refrigerate for 30 minutes.

Unwrap the pasta dough. Cut the dough into 4 equal portions and flatten each to a uniform thickness. Use a pasta machine or rolling pin to roll each portion into smooth 3-millimeter-thick pasta sheets measuring about 6 inches wide by 12 inches

WATCH THIS RECIPE

long to just cover the chitarra strings. If you don't have a chitarra, roll the pasta sheet and use a very sharp knife to cut it into strands measuring 12 inches long and 3 millimeters wide. Cover the sheets with a kitchen towel while you work to prevent them from drying out.

Uncover a sheet and dust it on one side. Place floured-side down over the wires of the chitarra. Dust all over with flour and use a rolling pin to press the pasta sheet through the wires. Roll over the pasta until the sheet has been sliced into strands. Collect the pasta from the compartment, from into a nest, and set it aside on a flour-dusted surface. Repeat with the remaining dough.

SFOGLIA VERDE

FRESH EGG AND SPINACH PASTA DOUGH

*Makes about 1¼ pounds
(4 servings)*

---

*Total prep and cooking time:
1 hour 30 minutes*

6 ounces fresh spinach,
blanched, or 2 ounces frozen
spinach, thawed and drained

195 grams (3 to 4 large) eggs,
at room temperature

300 grams (about 1¾ cups plus
2 tablespoons) all-purpose or
OO flour, plus more for dusting

GORGEOUS TIP

Blanching the fresh spinach
(putting it briefly in boiling
salted water), makes it tender
and preserves its color. Bring
a large pot of water to a rolling
boil over high heat. Season with
salt until it tastes like a seasoned
soup, add the spinach and boil
until the stems become tender,
about 2 minutes. Drain, cool,
and squeeze out any liquid using
cheesecloth or a kitchen towel.

Sfoglia verde is a pasta sheet tinted a brilliant green color
with spinach. It makes a gorgeous pairing with vegetables in
a layered Lasagna Vegetariana (page 136), but you could also
use it to make ravioli. The original lasagna bolognese recipe
from the northern Italian region of Emilia also uses sfoglia
verde, although most meaty lasagnas outside that region call
for a simple golden Sfoglia all'Uovo (page 9). For an authentic
Bolognese flair, use sfoglia verde instead of sfoglia all'uovo
when making Lasagna al Ragù di Lady Caterina (page 71).
Follow the Pasta Machine Instructions on page 10, but if you
wish to roll by hand, see Rolling Pasta by Hand on page 12.

In a food processor, combine the spinach and eggs and blend
until the mixture is very smooth, about 30 seconds.

Pour the flour onto your work surface and make a well in the
center using a spoon or your hands. Pour the spinach and egg
mixture into the well and gently mix together with a fork. Little
by little and working from the inside of the well to the edges,
bring some flour into the spinach and egg mixture, stirring with
a fork until each portion of flour is incorporated. When the
spinach and egg mixture is no longer runny, begin kneading
the dough with your hands, feeling how it changes beneath
your fingertips as you work.

Use your whole body to rock back and forth over the dough,
pressing it against your work surface until the eggs and flour
have become one. Continue kneading to strengthen the dough
for 10 minutes longer, massaging it forcefully, until it is strong
and glossy and it springs back when you press a finger into it.
Wrap tightly with plastic wrap and refrigerate for 30 minutes.

Unwrap the pasta dough. Cut the dough into 4 equal portions
and flatten each to a uniform thickness. Run each dough
piece through a pasta machine, starting on the widest
setting and repeating on successively thinner settings until
it is almost transparent. Pasta machines typically make long
sheets 6 inches wide.

For lasagna: Cut the pasta sheet into pieces that fit your baking dish. Assemble the lasagna according to the instructions on page 36. You do not need to cook the pasta in advance; it will cook as it bakes.

Homemade POTATO GNOCCHI

*Makes about 1¼ pounds
(4 servings)*

———

*Total prep and cooking time:
2 hours 15 minutes*

680 grams/about 1½ pounds
starchy potatoes (I like russets)

150 grams (about 1 cup)
all-purpose flour, plus more
for dusting

Sea salt

1 large egg yolk, at room
temperature

Potato gnocchi was the first pasta shape I learned to make. In fact, it was the very first thing I ever learned to cook. Gently bringing together potatoes, flour, and a bit of salt to make a pillowy and delicate dumpling to serve alla Sorrentina (see page 56) or with butter and sage (see page 190) is very simple and relaxing. The trick to making the perfect gnocchi is to use very dry potatoes. I use russets that have been in my pantry for a month or two, and I never make gnocchi from freshly purchased potatoes if I can help it. Moist potatoes require more flour, and therefore more kneading, which makes the consistency gluey and dense versus the light, ethereal *gnocco* I love to serve.

Place the potatoes in a medium pot and cover them with cold water. Bring to a boil over high heat. Reduce the heat to medium-low and simmer until the potatoes are easily pierced with a knife, about 45 minutes.

Drain the potatoes, let cool, and peel. Pass them through a potato ricer. Transfer to a clean work surface, then sprinkle the flour and a heavy pinch of salt over the potatoes. Gently fold the potatoes and flour together just until they come together. Use your fingers or a spoon to make a well in the center of the mixture. Add the egg yolk to the well and gently beat it with a fork. Little by little, working from the inside of the well to the edges, bring some flour into the egg mixture, stirring with the fork until each portion of flour is incorporated. When the egg mixture is no longer runny, begin kneading the dough with your hands until no dry flour bits remain.

Sprinkle some flour over a baking sheet or a plate.

Uncover the dough and cut off an egg-sized piece. Roll it into a ¾-inch-thick rope. Use a sharp knife or dough scraper to cut the rope crosswise into 1-inch pieces. Repeat with the remaining dough. If you wish, roll each piece over a gnocchi board or the tines of a fork to create a ridged texture. Set aside on the flour-dusted baking sheet.

WATCH THIS RECIPE

Bring a medium pot of water to a rolling boil over high heat. Season with salt until it tastes like a seasoned soup.

Working in batches, boil the gnocchi until they float and are tender, 2 to 2½ minutes. Drain and set aside on a clean baking sheet or plate (if you reuse the baking sheet from before, be sure to wipe off any flour).

If you don't plan to eat the gnocchi that day, cover the baking sheet with plastic wrap and place the uncooked gnocchi in the freezer for 30 minutes, then uncover and gently slide the gnocchi into a freezer bag. You can keep the gnocchi in the freezer for up to 2 months. To thaw them, take them out 30 minutes before you plan to cook them.

GORGEOUS TIPS

While you might find larger potato gnocchi in Rome, I always make mine on the smaller side, ¾ inch by 1 inch. I find that size is perfect for creating the right balance of sauce and pasta, so one doesn't overpower the other. The goal is always balance.

Potato gnocchi can be formed by simply slicing pieces from a rope of dough, leaving the exterior smooth. You can also give them a ridged texture by rolling them over a gnocchi board or the tines of a fork. Either will leave a wavy impression in the gnocchi, which gives the sauce more surface area to cling to.

TORTELLINI

Makes about 1 pound
(4 servings)

———

Total prep and cooking time:
1 hour 30 minutes

Pasta

300 grams (about 1¾ cups
plus 2 tablespoons) all-purpose
or 00 flour

195 grams (3 to 4 large) eggs,
at room temperature

Filling

1 tablespoon butter

3½ ounces pork loin

½ sprig rosemary, picked

½ sprig thyme, picked

3½ ounces Prosciutto di Parma,
roughly chopped

3½ ounces mortadella,
roughly chopped

1 large egg

Freshly grated nutmeg

½ teaspoon freshly ground
black pepper

100 grams/3½ ounces
(about 1¼ cups) finely grated
Parmigiano-Reggiano

Tortellini originally come from the northern Italian region of Emilia, a place of rich cuisines drenched in luxurious ingredients like Parmigiano-Reggiano and Aceto Balsamico Tradizionale. These gorgeous pasta parcels are made from Sfoglia all'Uovo (page 9) and pinched by expert hands into impossibly tiny tortellini. The traditional filling for tortellini is a mixture of meats that is seasoned with salty cheese, and its natural pairings are a cream sauce enriched with Parmigiano-Reggiano, as in Tortellini alla Panna (page 131), or in an earthy meat broth like Tortellini in Brodo (page 145). You can also make slightly larger filled pasta called tortelloni, which are stuffed with ricotta-based fillings (see Tortelloni Fillings, pages 23–24).

Make the pasta: Pour the flour onto your work surface and use your fingers or a spoon to make a well in the center. Crack the eggs into the well and gently beat them together with a fork. Little by little, working from the inside of the well to the edges, bring some flour into the egg mixture, stirring with the fork until each portion of flour is incorporated. When the egg mixture is no longer runny, begin kneading the dough with your hands, feeling how it changes beneath your fingertips as you work.

Use your whole body to rock back and forth over the dough, pressing it against your work surface and away from you until the eggs and flour have become one. Continue kneading to strengthen the dough, working it over like a lover, until it is strong and glossy and it springs back when you press a finger into it. Wrap tightly with plastic wrap and refrigerate for 30 minutes.

Unwrap the pasta dough. Cut the dough into 4 equal portions and flatten each to a uniform thickness. Run each dough piece through your pasta machine, starting on the widest setting and repeating on successively thinner settings until it is almost transparent. Pasta machines typically make long sheets 6 inches wide. (If rolling by hand, see Rolling Pasta by Hand, page 12.)

recipe continues

Prepare the filling: Melt the butter in a small pan over medium heat, then add the pork loin, rosemary, and thyme and cook until the pork begins to brown, 5 to 7 minutes. Remove from the heat. Cut the meat into small pieces.

Combine the cooked pork loin, rosemary, thyme, prosciutto, and mortadella in a food processor and blend into a paste.

In a medium bowl, combine the meat mixture, egg, a pinch of nutmeg, the pepper, and Parmigiano-Reggiano. Mix together until well incorporated. Set aside, covered, in the refrigerator for at least 12 hours.

To cut the tortellini, use a sharp knife to cut the pasta sheets into 1¼-inch squares. Set aside any irregular pieces to use as maltagliati.

To fill the tortellini, place a dab of filling about the size of a pea in the center of each pasta square. Keep the rest of the pasta squares covered with a kitchen towel while you work.

To shape the tortellini, pick up a single pasta piece by the filling, which will adhere to the pasta, and rest it on the place where your middle and index finger meet your palm. Using the thumb and index finger of the opposite hand, fold two opposite ends together to form a triangle and press to close. Working with one edge at a time, seal the other edges closed using your thumb and index finger.

Gently grip one tip of the pasta with your thumb and index finger, letting the filled pasta drape over your extended index finger. Wrap the opposite tip of the pasta around your index finger and join it to the tip with your thumb and index finger.

Place the shaped *tortellino* on a clean, dry work surface. Repeat with the remaining dough and filling.

Bring a large pot of water to a rolling boil over high heat. Season with salt until the water tastes like a seasoned soup. Drop in the tortellini, working in batches if needed to avoid overcrowding the pot, and cook until they float and are tender, 2 to 3 minutes.

GORGEOUS TIP

When you pinch the tortellini closed, you are doubling the thickness in the places where the pasta sheets meet, which means those parts will cook more slowly than the single layer enveloping the filling. When you use your fingertips to press the tortellini closed, press until the pasta is as thin as a single layer.

TORTELLONI FILLINGS:
Tradition calls for meat filling in tortellini, but for slightly larger tortelloni (see opposite), you can really get creative and make any filling you want based on your mood and what cheeses and vegetables you have in your pantry. Find your own perfect sauce pairings to go with whichever pasta fillings your appetite desires.

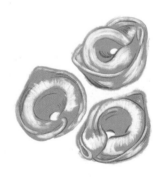

Ricotta and Lemon Zest Tortelloni Filling

Makes enough for 1 recipe tortelloni

Pasta dough (from Tortellini, page 21)

1 cup fresh ricotta, drained

Grated zest of 1 lemon

1 large egg

60 grams/2 ounces (about ¾ cup) finely grated Parmigiano-Reggiano

Sea salt

Make the pasta dough as directed and follow the instructions up to "To cut the tortellini." Using a sharp knife or accordion pastry cutter, cut the sheet into 2- to 2½-inch squares.

In a food processor, combine the ricotta, lemon zest, egg, Parmigiano-Reggiano, and a heavy pinch of salt and blend until smooth, about 30 seconds. (Alternatively, mix the ingredients together vigorously by hand in a medium bowl.)

Transfer to a pastry bag or sturdy plastic bag with one corner trimmed off and pipe a marble-sized amount of the filling onto the center of each pasta piece. Cover the rest of the pasta squares with a kitchen towel while you shape to prevent them from drying out.

Follow the instructions for shaping and cooking in Tortellini (see page 22).

Ricotta and Nutmeg Tortelloni Filling

Makes enough for 1 recipe tortelloni

Pasta dough (from Tortellini, page 21)

1 cup fresh ricotta, drained

½ teaspoon freshly grated nutmeg

1 large egg

60 grams/2 ounces (about ¾ cup) finely grated Parmigiano-Reggiano

Sea salt

Make the pasta dough as directed in Tortellini (page 21) and follow the instructions up to "To cut the tortellini." Using a sharp knife or accordion pastry cutter, cut the sheet into 2- to 2½-inch squares.

In a food processor, combine the ricotta, nutmeg, egg, Parmigiano-Reggiano, and a heavy pinch of salt and blend until very smooth, about 30 seconds. (Alternatively, mix the ingredients together vigorously by hand in a medium bowl.)

Transfer to a pastry bag or sturdy plastic bag with one corner trimmed off and pipe a marble-sized amount of the filling onto the center of each pasta piece. Cover the rest of the pasta squares with a kitchen towel while you shape to prevent them from drying out.

Follow the instructions for shaping and cooking in Tortellini (see page 22).

recipe continues

Ricotta and Mushroom Tortelloni Filling

Makes enough for 1 recipe tortelloni

Pasta dough (from Tortellini, page 21)

3 ounces mushrooms (I like cremini), cut or torn into bite-sized pieces

1 tablespoon extra-virgin olive oil

Sea salt and freshly ground black pepper

2 sprigs fresh thyme

¾ cup fresh ricotta, drained

1 large egg

Sea salt

Preheat the oven to 425°F.

Make the pasta dough as directed in Tortellini (page 21) and follow the instructions up to "To cut the tortellini." Using a sharp knife or accordion pastry cutter, cut the sheet into 2- to 2½-inch squares.

On a sheet pan, toss the mushrooms, olive oil, a heavy pinch of salt, a scrunch of pepper, and thyme and spread out evenly. Roast until golden and caramelized, about 15 minutes. Discard the thyme.

In a food processor, combine the mushrooms and any pan juices, the ricotta, egg, and a heavy pinch of salt and blend until very smooth, about 30 seconds. (Alternatively, mix the ingredients together vigorously by hand in a medium bowl.)

Transfer to a pastry bag or sturdy plastic bag with one corner trimmed off and pipe a marble-sized amount of the filling onto the center of each pasta piece. Cover the rest of the pasta squares with a kitchen towel while you shape to prevent them from drying out.

Follow the instructions for shaping and cooking in Tortellini (page 22).

Zio Franco, center, living life to the fullest at one of the more modest Munno family gatherings.

RAVIOLI

Makes about 32 ravioli
(4 servings)

———

Total prep and cooking time:
1 hour 30 minutes

Pasta

300 grams (about 1¼ cups
plus 2 tablespoons) all-purpose
or 00 flour

195 grams (3 to 4 large) eggs,
at room temperature

Filling

250 grams/9 ounces fresh ricotta,
drained

200 grams/7 ounces spinach,
blanched and roughly chopped

80 grams/3 ounces (about 1 cup)
finely grated Parmigiano-Reggiano

Sea salt

Ravioli are sealed pasta parcels that come in assorted shapes: square, round, or half-moons. I prefer a square *raviolo*—when you cut round or half-moon ones, the excess dough makes a lot of scraps and therefore fewer ravioli. The classic Italian raviolo filling is ricotta and spinach and, while it is rather delicate, you often find it served with a punchy Fresh Tomato Sauce (page 155) or even a light coating of Ragù di Lady Caterina (page 64). I personally favor an herb-infused butter sauce (see page 190), which I believe complements rather than overwhelms the ricotta filling. See page 29 for different ravioli fillings to choose whichever you fancy for the sauce you are making.

Make the pasta: Pour the flour onto your work surface and use your fingers or a spoon to make a well in the center. Crack the eggs into the well and gently beat them together with a fork. Little by little and working from the inside of the well to the edges, bring some flour into the egg mixture, stirring with the fork until each portion of flour is incorporated. When the egg mixture is no longer runny, begin kneading the dough with your hands, feeling how it changes beneath your fingertips as you work.

Use your whole body to rock back and forth over the dough, pressing it against your work surface and away from you until the eggs and flour have become one. Continue kneading to strengthen the dough, energetically caressing it, until it is strong and glossy and it springs back when you press a finger into it. Wrap tightly with plastic wrap and refrigerate for 30 minutes.

Unwrap the pasta dough. Cut the dough into 4 equal portions and flatten each to a uniform thickness. Run each dough piece through your pasta machine, starting on the widest setting and repeating on successively thinner settings until it is almost transparent. Pasta machines typically make long sheets up to 6 inches wide. Cut the sheet into 4 × 12-inch pieces. (If rolling by hand, follow the instructions in Rolling Pasta by Hand, page 12, then cut the pasta into 4 × 12-inch pieces.)

recipe continues

Make the filling: In a food processor, combine the ricotta, spinach, Parmigiano-Reggiano, and a pinch of salt and blend until smooth, about 30 seconds. (Alternatively, mix the ingredients together vigorously by hand in a medium bowl.)

To fill the ravioli, use your fingers and a spoon to place about ¾ tablespoon of filling ½ inch from the edge of one long side of the dough. Repeat every inch for a total of 6 tablespoons across the sheet.

To seal the ravioli, spray a mist of water over the pasta and filling to help the pasta layers stick together. Fold the dough in half lengthwise and press the pasta sheets together and around the filling to seal each raviolo. Use a pasta cutting wheel or a sharp knife to cut the ravioli into 2-inch squares.

Bring a large pot of water to a rolling boil over high heat. Season with salt until the water tastes like a seasoned soup. Drop in the ravioli in batches if necessary to avoid overcrowding the pot and cook until they float and are tender, 2½ to 3 minutes.

Ricotta and Mushroom Filling

Makes enough for 1 recipe ravioli

———

1 tablespoon unsalted butter

7 ounces mushrooms (I like cremini), roughly chopped

1 sprig fresh thyme

Sea salt

1¼ cups fresh ricotta, drained

80 grams/3 ounces (about 1 cup) finely grated Parmigiano-Reggiano

1 large egg

In a medium skillet, melt the butter over medium heat until it is frothy and golden, about 30 seconds. Add the mushrooms, thyme, and a heavy pinch of salt. Cook until the mushrooms begin to caramelize, about 15 minutes. Discard the thyme. Once they are cool enough to handle, chop the mushrooms into tiny pieces.

In a food processor, combine the mushrooms, ricotta, Parmigiano-Reggiano, egg, and a pinch of salt and blend until smooth, about 30 seconds. (Alternatively, mix the ingredients together vigorously in a medium bowl.)

The filling will keep, refrigerated, in a sealed container for up to 3 days.

Fill and cook the ravioli as directed on page 28.

Butternut Squash and Provolone Filling

Makes enough for 1 recipe ravioli

———

200 grams/7 ounces butternut squash, cut into ½-inch cubes

2 tablespoons extra-virgin olive oil

Sea salt and freshly ground black pepper

200 grams/7 ounces fresh ricotta, drained

60 grams/2 ounces provolone, coarsely grated

60 grams/2 ounces (about ¾ cup) finely grated Parmigiano-Reggiano

1 large egg

Preheat the oven to 425°F.

On a sheet pan, toss the squash with the olive oil, a heavy pinch of salt, and a scrunch of pepper and spread out evenly. Roast until golden and caramelized, about 40 minutes.

In a food processor, combine the squash and any pan juices, the ricotta, provolone, Parmigiano-Reggiano, a heavy pinch of salt, and the egg and blend until smooth, about 30 seconds. (Alternatively, mash the squash, then mix the ingredients together vigorously in a medium bowl.)

The filling will keep, refrigerated, in a sealed container for up to 3 days.

Fill and cook the ravioli as directed on page 28.

PASTA ACQUA E FARINA

FLOUR AND WATER DOUGH
FOR ORECCHIETTE

*Makes about 1 pound
(4 servings)*

———

*Total prep and cooking time:
1 hour 15 minutes*

300 grams semolina, plus more
for dusting

150 grams (a little less than ⅔ cup)
lukewarm water

This dough is made from durum wheat, which grows abundantly in Southern Italy, especially the high plains that straddle Campania and Puglia. It is typically used to make short, hand-formed pasta shapes like *orecchiette*, which means "little ears" in Italian, so named because of their funny anatomical form. My stepmother, Angela, is from Puglia, so I first got to know the pasta shape through her when I was about six. When my father married Angela we acquired another nonna, Michelina, a fabulous cook and tireless pasta maker. I love to prepare orecchiette in her style, served in a light broccoli rabe and sausage sauce (see page 174) or tossed with cacioricotta and tomato sauce (see page 160). The pasta's shape is perfect for scooping up sauces in the most adorable way.

Pour the flour into a shallow bowl and make a well in the center using a spoon or your hands. Pour the water into the well. Little by little and working from the inside of the well to the edges, bring some flour into the water, stirring with a fork until each portion of flour is incorporated. When the water has been mostly absorbed, turn the dough out onto your work surface and knead it with your hands, feeling how it changes beneath your fingertips as you work.

Use your whole body to rock back and forth over the dough, pressing it against your work surface until the water and flour have become one. Continue kneading to strengthen the dough, working it over like a lover, until it is strong and it springs back when you press a finger into it. Wrap with plastic wrap and refrigerate for 30 minutes.

For orecchiette: Cut off an egg-sized piece of dough and roll it into a rope about ¼ inch thick. Using a dull knife, press into the dough about ½ inch from the one end of the dough rope and use the knife to drag the small piece of dough across the work surface. Turn the piece inside out by inverting it on your thumb. Set aside on a baking sheet or plate dusted with semolina. Repeat with the remaining dough to shape more orecchiette.

CHAPTER TWO

WHERE IT ALL BEGAN

The Classics

I learned to cook in my nonna's kitchen near Naples, where I spent many hours standing on an old wicker chair watching fresh tomato sauce bubbling away on the stove.

Between the aromas, the heat, and the sparkle of pride in my nonna's eye, I couldn't have been happier. It was there I learned to make Lasagna di Lady Caterina (page 71), Pasta e Fagioli con Pasta Mista Corta (page 60), and Spaghettoni alla Puttanesca (page 68), not to mention an important lesson: If you really want to show someone you love them, you cook for them from scratch using the best ingredients you can find, along with plenty of patience and passion.

My family moved away when it was time for me to go to school, shortly after my parents separated. All of a sudden, I found myself on a Rome-bound train with my mom and my younger brother, Agostino (aka Pasta Bro). I was heartbroken, and my life changed overnight. I missed the huge family meals and the intense affection that poured across the table at my nonna's, especially from my grandparents and aunts. I craved a big family with lots of love around me. With an incredibly hardworking mother who put in late hours, it was sometimes up to me to feed Agostino. Even though it was just the two of us, I tried to make each meal special. Fortunately, I was able to return to my family down south for a few months each year, and even though I missed spending time with my nonna, it made the time we did get to spend together all the more special.

As I got older, I began to eat out at local *trattorie*, classic Roman eateries that aren't just casual restaurants with a simple menu—they're an entire universe. I really love the atmosphere of a family-run trattoria. They always have all their kids there; aunts, uncles, and cousins are constantly popping in and out, and regulars become part of a big, lively family. It's a gorgeous and distinctly Roman space full of food, love, and family—the most important things. These trattorias became a second family to me and the perfect substitute for my nonna's kitchen. It was there I learned the Roman classics that I dutifully reproduced at home.

My own cooking during this time either involved my nonna's recipes or Roman classics. Those formative flavors are the ones you will find in this chapter: tomatoes, chili peppers, capers, and salted anchovies of Southern Italy, and the Pecorino Romano and guanciale that are icons in Rome. In Italy, each city and village has its own unique specialties, and each region is like its own country when it comes to food. Yet, as distinct as they are, Rome's and Capua's dishes are right at home together in this chapter, beautifully complementing one another across regional borders. Both shaped my passion for food and cooking, an intense desire to share it with the people I love, and my need to build a family around it.

TONNARELLI CACIO E PEPE

TONNARELLI WITH
PECORINO ROMANO AND
BLACK PEPPER

Serves 4

Total prep and cooking time:
15 minutes

Alternate pasta shape:
spaghetti

300 grams/10½ ounces
(about 3¾ cups) finely ground
Pecorino Romano

1 tablespoon coarsely ground
black pepper, plus more for garnish

Sea salt

1 pound homemade Tonnarelli
(page 14) or store-bought fresh
spaghetti alla chitarra

Cacio e pepe is the dish that's followed me throughout my entire life; from the dinner table as a small child to the hectic trattoria down the street to standing around the stove with friends after a night at the *discoteca*, cacio e pepe has been a constant presence. It's earthy, silky, simple, and satisfying—and, perhaps best of all, it comes together fast.

Don't let the simplicity of cacio e pepe's ingredients fool you. This recipe, perhaps more than any other in this book, requires some practice. The perfect cacio e pepe is all about creating a silky sauce that mingles with pasta strands without clumping. This means carefully managing the ingredients, timing, and heat to create maximum lusciousness. My secret for achieving this is to use a moist, young Pecorino Romano around nine months old rather than a drier, aged one. I use the small punched holes of a box grater to create a powdery flurry of cheese ideal for melting evenly, and I boil the pasta in half the amount of water as I usually would for maximum starch content. I also use very little salt in the water, since Pecorino Romano is already very salty. All of these tricks conspire to guarantee each strand is bound in a creamy marriage with the pecorino and black pepper sauce.

Fill a large pot halfway with water. Bring the water to a rolling boil over high heat.

While the water is coming to a boil, in a medium bowl, combine the Pecorino Romano and 1 cup water and stir passionately, adding more water a little at a time as needed, to make a luscious cream.

In a large skillet, heat the ground pepper over low heat, swirling to lightly toast it and bring out its gorgeous aromas, about 30 seconds. Add a splash of water and swirl to infuse it with the pepper's spicy and smoky aromatics. Remove the pan from the heat.

recipe continues

WATCH THIS RECIPE

Once the water has reached a rolling boil, season lightly with salt. Drop in the tonnarelli and cook until the pasta is tender, 2 to 2½ minutes.

Transfer the pasta directly to the skillet with the pepper. Pour in the Pecorino Romano sauce and toss vigorously until the pasta is drenched in peppery sauce and the sauce is silky and smooth. Add the tears of the gods a spoonful at a time if the sauce is clumpy and stir passionately until smooth.

Serve drizzled with any remaining sauce in the skillet and garnish with a scrunch of pepper.

GORGEOUS TIPS

Cacio e Pepe is a very fast recipe to make because the tonnarelli cook so quickly and the sauce isn't cooked. Using the tears of the gods in the Pecorino Romano sauce is essential for breaking down the cheese's proteins and creating a silky outcome.

Coarsely grinding peppercorns awakens their flavors and brings a subtle smokiness to your cacio e pepe. Be sure to always use fresh peppercorns—they should taste spicy when you bite into them— and grind them just before you begin to cook.

Be confident and a bit aggressive while mixing the pasta with the sauce. Use two wooden spoons and toss with the passion of an Italian until the pasta and sauce form a velvety union.

SPAGHETTI *alla* CARBONARA

SPAGHETTI WITH GUANCIALE, PECORINO ROMANO, AND BLACK PEPPER

Serves 4

Total prep and cooking time: 20 minutes

Alternate pasta shapes:
rigatoni, spaghetti alla chitarra

6 ounces guanciale, cut into 1 × ½ × ½-inch sticks

4 large egg yolks

1 large egg

140 grams/5 ounces (about 1¾ cups) finely grated Pecorino Romano, plus more for dusting

2 teaspoons freshly ground black pepper, plus more for garnish

Sea salt

1 pound spaghetti

WATCH THIS RECIPE

Carbonara is THE Roman pasta dish. And that is for good reason. It's a beautifully emulsified sauce of eggs, guanciale, Pecorino Romano cheese, and black pepper—strong flavors that drip in decadence. It's precisely this decadence that supports my theory for carbonara's origins. Perhaps you have heard the various myths surrounding carbonara's birth. Just a few of the stories are: 1) Roman trattoria owners invented it to satisfy American soldiers' demand for bacon and eggs after World War II. 2) It was created by the *carbonari* (charcoal makers), the black pepper recalling the black dust that settled on their clothes while working. 3) It was the signature dish of a secret society called the Carbonari that would feast on it at their clandestine meetings. I like to think it was invented by a clever cook in the late 1950s—this is, after all, when the first true written record for carbonara appeared—who was eager to assert Rome's hunger for luxury after a difficult war time, mixing an egg into the classic and beloved Gricia (page 46). We may never know the real origins of carbonara, but we can crack the code on its silky sauce. The trick to the creamiest carbonara you have ever had is pasta water, using it to temper the eggs (see Tempering Eggs, page 40), emulsify the guanciale fat, and bind it together. Just like with Cacio e Pepe (page 36), it's essential to get physical with your carbonara, stirring vigorously to create a sauce that's as decadent as it is timeless.

Bring a large pot of water to a rolling boil over high heat.

Meanwhile, in a large deep sauté pan, heat the guanciale over low heat and sizzle until golden and lightly crispy, about 10 minutes. Remove from the heat and transfer three-quarters of the guanciale and its luscious fat to a large bowl to cool. Set aside the remaining guanciale on a paper towel to use as garnish. Keep the pan in reserve.

recipe continues

GORGEOUS TIPS

Once the guanciale fat has cooled to the point it won't scramble the eggs when it comes into contact with them, add the egg yolks, whole egg, Pecorino Romano, and black pepper to the bowl, beating passionately to make a thick and creamy sauce.

Once the water has reached a rolling boil, season with salt until it tastes like a seasoned soup. Drop in the pasta and cook until al dente.

Transfer the pasta to the pan where the guanciale was cooked.

Add a ladle (½ cup) of pasta cooking water to the egg mixture 1 tablespoon at a time and beat energetically to combine. Pour the egg mixture over the pasta. Stir passionately until the sauce thickens, adding more pasta water as needed 1 tablespoon at a time until you reach the perfect consistency.

Serve garnished with a scrunch of black pepper, a dusting of Pecorino Romano, and the reserved guanciale pieces sprinkled on top.

Guanciale is currently the go-to cured pork ingredient for carbonara. But the ingredients weren't always so cut and dried. People used what they had, so in that spirit, feel free to reach for pancetta or even bacon as you make my carbonara your own.

The amount of rendered guanciale fat in this recipe depends on the type of guanciale you are using. Typically, American guanciale emits far less fat than Italian-made. If the guanciale releases just a few tablespoons of fat, you are good to go. If you see there is ½ cup or more in the pan, I recommend draining some off and discarding the excess. Use your judgment to strike a balance between a nice fat content and going overboard.

TEMPERING EGGS

Eggs are a beautiful mix of fat (the yolk) and protein (the white) that can be finessed into a smooth and creamy mixture through a process called tempering. By adding some hot liquid—pasta water, in this case—to the egg, guanciale, and Pecorino Romano mixture and stirring vigorously, the eggs are gently warmed by the water, which prevents scrambling and lends to a creamy consistency to the finished sauce.

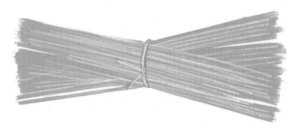

GORGEOUS TIP

For this recipe I like to use a
potato masher to smash the
tomatoes directly into the sauce,
but you can crush them by hand
(see page 58) before adding them
to the pan if you wish.

SPAGHETTI *all'*AMATRICIANA

SPAGHETTI WITH
TOMATO, GUANCIALE, AND
PECORINO ROMANO

Serves 4

Total prep and cooking time:
25 minutes

Alternate pasta shapes:
bucatini, mezze maniche
(half rigatoni), rigatoni,
potato gnocchi

1 tablespoon extra-virgin olive oil

5 ounces guanciale or pancetta, cut
into 1 × ½ × ½-inch sticks

½ cup dry white wine

1 (28-ounce) can whole peeled
tomatoes

Sea salt

2 dried chili peppers (I like cayenne
and Calabrian chilies)

1 pound spaghetti

100 grams/3½ ounces
(about 1¼ cups) finely grated
Pecorino Romano, plus more
for dusting

Amatriciana sauce is a staple in Rome and all over the Lazio region, but one city claims to be its birthplace: Amatrice. This mountain village of stone houses has a famous pork-curing tradition dating back thousands of years, and the guanciale (cured pork jowl) and pancetta (cured pork belly) from this area are just gorgeous. The Amatriciana recipe is a traditional one that the people of Amatrice fiercely defend. In fact, the city hall keeps the official recipe on record and lists the ingredients: spaghetti, guanciale, extra-virgin olive oil, white wine, whole peeled tomatoes, chili pepper, Pecorino Romano, and salt.

There's furious debate in Rome and generally in Lazio over which cured pork to use (guanciale, pancetta, or smoked pancetta), whether to flavor it with garlic or onion (the official recipe uses neither of these), and whether to use black pepper, chili pepper, or no spices at all. I mainly stick to the rules from Amatrice in my own kitchen, but I love trying other versions. No matter what, you will have a sauce that is earthy, hearty, and rich with flavor.

Bring a large pot of water to a rolling boil over high heat.

Meanwhile, in a large deep sauté pan, heat the olive oil, guanciale, and chili peppers over medium-low heat and sizzle until the guanciale is golden and aromatic, 5 to 7 minutes. Add the wine, increase the heat to medium-high, and cook until the alcohol aroma evaporates and the liquid reduces by half, about 1½ minutes. Set aside the guanciale and discard the chili peppers.

Add the tomatoes and smash them with a potato masher. Once the tomatoes have cooked for a few minutes, add the guanciale, reserving a few pieces per person for garnish, and season with salt to taste. Some guanciale is very salty, so be more cautious with salt seasoning than usual until you get to know this ingredient. Simmer, gently stirring, for 5 minutes longer to marry the flavors of the sauce.

When the water has reached a rolling boil, season with salt until the water tastes like a seasoned soup. Drop in the pasta and cook until al dente.

recipe continues

Transfer the pasta to the sauce. Stir in the Pecorino Romano, then add a ladle (½ cup) of pasta cooking water and cook the pasta in the sauce, stirring energetically, and add more pasta cooking water as needed to finish cooking the pasta and create a luscious sauce.

Serve dusted with more Pecorino Romano and garnished with the reserved guanciale.

RIGATONI *alla* GRICIA

❋

RIGATONI WITH GUANCIALE,
PECORINO ROMANO,
AND BLACK PEPPER

Serves 4

———

Total prep and cooking time:
25 minutes

———

Alternate pasta shapes:
spaghetti, tonnarelli, mezze maniche,
bucatini

7 ounces guanciale, cut into
1 × ½ × ½-inch sticks

1 cup dry white wine (optional)

Sea salt

1 pound rigatoni

1 teaspoon freshly ground black
pepper, plus more for garnish

80 grams/3 ounces (about 1 cup)
finely grated Pecorino Romano,
plus more for dusting

Gricia is an unnoticed beauty, simple yet powerful in flavor. She often goes undetected. For Romans, she is one of the pillars of pasta, but foreigners know little about her, focusing more intensely on decadent carbonara (see page 39) and enticing Amatriciana (see page 43). Yet gricia is an ancestor to them both. Subtract egg from the carbonara and tomato from Amatriciana and you have the basics of gricia: pasta, guanciale, Pecorino Romano, and black pepper. These simple ingredients were easy to assemble at the working-class taverns and mobile food stalls that used to travel through the city to feed the urban poor more than a century ago. Eventually, gricia made its way onto trattoria menus and that's where I first encountered it. Osteria dei Pontefici, close to my childhood apartment near the Vatican, is still my first stop for gricia when I return to Rome. In just a few bites, this ancient Roman pasta dish signals to me that I am home.

Bring a large pot of water to a rolling boil over high heat.

Meanwhile, in a large deep sauté pan, heat the guanciale over medium heat until it is golden and aromatic and has released some of its fat, 5 to 7 minutes. Remove from the heat, scoop out the crispy guanciale with a slotted spoon, and place it in a bowl.

Once the rendered fat has cooled enough so it won't splatter when you add liquid, carefully add the wine (if using) to the skillet and cook over medium-high heat until the alcohol aroma dissipates and the liquid has reduced by half, about 1½ minutes.

Once the water has reached a rolling boil, season with salt until the water tastes like a seasoned soup. Drop in the pasta and cook until very al dente (a little more than half the recommended cooking time).

Transfer the pasta to the sauté pan along with a ladle (½ cup) of pasta cooking water and swirl the pasta until it is drenched in the wine-infused guanciale fat, cooking until al dente. Taste

frequently to determine when the pasta is done, adding more pasta cooking water as needed to keep the sauce creamy.

Add the black pepper, Pecorino Romano, and three-quarters of the guanciale to the pasta and stir passionately to marry the flavors.

Serve dusted with Pecorino Romano and garnished with the reserved guanciale and a scrunch of black pepper on top.

PENNE *all*'ARRABBIATA

❧

PENNE IN SPICY TOMATO SAUCE

Serves 4

———

Total prep and cooking time:
20 minutes

———

Alternate pasta shapes:
potato gnocchi, rigatoncini

¼ cup extra-virgin olive oil

2 garlic cloves, minced

3 fresh chili peppers (I like cayenne and Calabrian chilies), sliced into ⅛-inch rounds

1 tablespoon roughly chopped fresh parsley, plus more for garnish

1 (28-ounce) can whole peeled tomatoes, crushed by hand (see page 58)

Sea salt

1 pound penne

No dish gets my blood pumping like *penne all'arrabbiata,* a sultry pasta dish known for its spice and heat. I love the way the hot chili pepper flirts with acidic tomatoes in an intimate dance that is intensified by a flurry of chopped parsley. It jump-starts my heart every single time. My version is inspired by my friend Leo, who serves it with a mischievous grin at his Osteria dei Pontefici, my local favorite in Rome. Each time he places a dish of penne all'arrabbiata in front of me, I know it's going to taste of pure fire but it will be so good that I won't be able to stop eating it no matter how much it burns. He lets his tomato and chili pepper sauce bubble vigorously over an intense flame for just a few minutes so the flavors meld without the tomato losing its bright tang. Then he tosses the pasta into the sauce and infuses it with the heat of the chilies, cooling it all slightly with a sprinkling of fresh parsley.

You can modify your arrabbiata sauce using chilies that work with your preferred spice level. I use whole peperoncini, cayenne peppers, or Calabrian peppers, all of which are small red chili peppers with a brief and intense kick that is only moderately spicy by American standards—we are much more sensitive to spice in Italy! Get to know your chilies and find varieties that are available in your area. Taste them in their raw or dried form, cook with them, and see how they behave and what kind of heat they deliver. If you are very sensitive to spice, you can remove and seed the chilies for just a hint of heat.

Bring a large pot of water to a rolling boil over high heat.

In a large deep sauté pan, heat the olive oil, garlic, and chili peppers over medium-low heat and cook until the garlic starts sizzling with little bubbles around it, 1 to 2 minutes. Add the tomatoes with a heavy pinch of salt. Increase the heat to high and simmer passionately until the sauce begins to concentrate but has not yet lost its bright acidity, about 5 minutes.

Once the water has reached a rolling boil, season with salt until the water tastes like a seasoned soup. Drop in the

pasta and cook until very al dente (a little more than half the recommended cooking time).

Transfer the pasta to the sauté pan along with a ladle (½ cup) of pasta cooking water and the parsley and simmer, stirring tenderly, until the pasta is al dente. Taste frequently to determine when the pasta is done and add more pasta water as needed to finish cooking the pasta and keep the sauce loose. Serve garnished with a flurry of parsley.

SPAGHETTI AGLIO OLIO E PEPERONCINO

SPAGHETTI WITH GARLIC, OIL, AND CHILI PEPPER

Serves 4

Total prep and cooking time: 20 minutes

Alternate pasta shape:
spaghettoni

¾ cup extra-virgin olive oil

4 garlic cloves, minced

2 fresh chili peppers (I like cayenne and Calabrian chilies), sliced into ⅛-inch-thick rounds

Sea salt

1 pound spaghetti

WATCH THIS RECIPE

This dish announces its simplicity in its name: spaghetti with *aglio* (garlic), *olio* (extra-virgin olive oil), and *peperoncino* (chili pepper). There are very few ingredients, but I promise you, this dish is as satisfying as any elaborately assembled one. When I was a teenager, my best friend, Simona, and I would wipe ourselves out from studying, and by the time we walked home from school in Campo de' Fiori to her apartment near the Colosseum, we were delirious with hunger. We didn't even need to think to make aglio olio e peperoncino; the ingredients are staples in every Italian kitchen, and we could pull heaping plates together with little effort, restoring our empty stomachs with Italy's quickest pasta dish. Whether you're Italian or not, I encourage you to fold this pasta classic into your arsenal. Use the best oil you've got and don't skimp on it. Each strand of spaghetti should be coated in a glistening layer of it, threatening to leave traces of it on your lips and chin with every heaping forkful.

I like to cook the garlic for longer than usual to extract as much of its flavor as possible. That's why I add a splash of raw oil to the garlic as it cooks in the pan. It slows down and elongates the cooking process, which extracts all of the garlic essence that makes this a simple but powerful dish.

Bring a large pot of water to a rolling boil over high heat.

Meanwhile, in large deep sauté pan, heat ½ cup of the olive oil, the garlic, and chili peppers over medium-low heat and cook gently, adding 1 tablespoon of oil from the remaining ¼ cup every minute or so. Cook until the garlic starts sizzling with little bubbles around it, 1 to 2 minutes, then allow the oil to cool slightly. You want the oil to be very warm, but not sizzling hot, when you add the pasta.

recipe continues

Variations

Once the water has reached a rolling boil, season with salt until it tastes like seasoned soup. Drop in the pasta and cook until very al dente (a little more than half the recommended cooking time).

Transfer the pasta to the sauté pan along with a ladle (½ cup) of pasta cooking water. Increase the heat to medium-high, then toss with the passion of an Italian until the water is absorbed and the pasta is al dente, adding more pasta water as needed.

Serve.

NAPLES-INSPIRED VARIATION:
To give this recipe a sexy and savory Neapolitan flare, melt 2 or 3 salt-packed anchovy fillets into the oil with the garlic. Using the back of a wooden spoon, smash the anchovies into the warm oil until they vanish, infusing the oil with their gorgeous umami.

PUGLIA-INSPIRED VARIATION:
Italians never put cheese on aglio olio e peperoncino, but many southern Italians do add a savory topping of fried bread crumbs sprinkled on top. It has a similar seasoning effect, and it is just gorgeous. I learned this twist from my family in Puglia. To make your own fried bread crumbs, crumble the interior of a few slices of stale bread to the size of coffee grounds and season them with salt. Toast the bread crumbs in a bit of extra-virgin olive oil in a small skillet over medium-low heat until golden, and then sprinkle over the finished dish.

SPAGHETTI *alle* VONGOLE

SPAGHETTI WITH CLAMS

Serves 4

———

Total prep and cooking time:
25 minutes

———

Alternate pasta shapes:
linguine, spaghettoni

3 tablespoons extra-virgin olive oil

1 garlic clove, minced

2 pounds littleneck or Manila
clams, cleaned (see How to Clean
Clams, page 55)

1 cup dry white wine

1 tablespoon roughly chopped
fresh parsley leaves, plus more for
garnish

Sea salt

1 pound spaghetti

Spaghetti alle vongole is one of those dishes in Italy that transcends regional boundaries. While pasta alla Norma (see page 97) is undeniably Sicilian and Cacio e Pepe (page 36) is classically Roman, you'll find spaghetti with clams eaten with equal enthusiasm across every Italian region, especially on Fridays, when Catholic tradition once required people to eat fish instead of meat. That tradition may technically be over, but you'll find that Italians have a hard time letting go of the past. You'll generally see spaghetti with clams made *in bianco*, that is, without tomato sauce, although it's quite common around Naples at the peak of summer to add a small handful of grape or cherry tomatoes to the sauce for a little color and flavor.

The types of clams we use in Italy, especially the *vongole veraci* and *lupini* varieties, are impossible to find in the US, so my secret is to pick out the smallest littleneck or Manila clams I can find at my local fish market. You can also ask your fishmonger or supermarket deli staff to provide you with the smallest and sweetest clams they have. Regardless of your clam choice, what really makes this dish special is its beautifully emulsified sauce. The sauce is made by simmering the clam juice with extra-virgin olive oil and the tears of the gods, which releases its starchy magic into the pasta as it mingles with the flavors of the sea. To make this dish even creamier, use linguine instead of spaghetti (a fun tip I learned from a Neapolitan chef). The tapered edges of the linguine shred slightly as you stir, releasing even more silky starch into the sauce.

Bring a large pot of water to a rolling boil over high heat.

In a large deep sauté pan, heat the olive oil and garlic over medium-low heat and cook until the garlic starts sizzling with little bubbles around it, 1 to 2 minutes. Increase the heat to medium-high and add the clams and wine. Cook, uncovered, using tongs to transfer the clams to a medium bowl as soon as they open. Some clams will open within 30 seconds, others after about 3 minutes. Discard any clams that do not open. Stir

GORGEOUS TIP

While the pasta is cooking, I like to pick about three-quarters of the cooked clams out of their shells using a small fork. Then when I combine the cooked clams with the cooked pasta, there are enough shells for splitting among the dishes as a garnish of sorts, and it avoids overcrowding the pan during the cooking process.

in the parsley and remove from the heat. Pick about three-quarters of the clam meats from their shells, discarding the shells, and set aside. Leave the remaining clams as is.

Once the water has reached a rolling boil, season with salt until it tastes like a seasoned soup. Drop in the pasta and cook until very al dente (a little more than half the recommended cooking time).

Transfer the pasta to the pan with the clam cooking juices. Increase the heat to high and cook until the pasta is al dente, stirring frequently as it absorbs the liquid. Check frequently to see when the pasta is done and add more pasta cooking water as needed to finish cooking the pasta and keep the sauce loose.

Just before serving the pasta, add all of the cooked clams to the pan and toss well to warm them.

Serve with parsley sprinkled on top.

HOW TO CLEAN CLAMS

Clams can be quite sandy, so be sure to purge them before you start cooking. Rinse the clams, tossing out any with broken shells, then soak in cold, salted water in the refrigerator for 30 minutes to 1 hour to purge any remaining sand. Drain in a colander and rinse before cooking.

GNOCCHI *alla* SORRENTINA

POTATO GNOCCHI
BAKED WITH TOMATO
AND CHEESE

Serves 4

---

*Total prep and cooking time:
30 minutes*

3 tablespoons extra-virgin olive oil

2 garlic cloves, minced

6 fresh basil leaves, torn, plus whole
leaves for garnish

1 (28-ounce) can whole peeled
tomatoes, crushed by hand
(see page 58)

Sea salt

Homemade Potato Gnocchi
(page 18) or 1¼ pounds
store-bought gnocchi

5 ounces mozzarella, torn into
1-inch pieces

60 grams/2 ounces (about ¾ cup)
finely grated Parmigiano-Reggiano

WATCH THIS RECIPE

Plump potato dumplings are the pillowy partners of tomato, basil, and cheese in this baked pasta dish named for the seaside town of Sorrento. Like many children in Campania, I grew up eating hearty *gnocchi alla sorrentina* in my Nonna Caterina's kitchen, which was not so far from the dish's namesake. During cold weather, my nonna would gently bring together potato and flour dough to make gnocchi, and then combine the pasta with a quick tomato sauce and bake it with two cheeses for the ultimate comfort meal. Even as an adult, I still eat this when I need a taste of home, and it never fails to satisfy my nostalgia for Nonna Caterina's cooking.

The heat of the oven gives this dish the ultimate combination of gorgeousness: a bit of crust from the Parmigiano-Reggiano and a sensual cheese pull from the mozzarella. Each bite feels like a warm ray of Sorrentine sunshine on a winter day.

Preheat the oven to 450°F.

Bring a large pot of water to a rolling boil over high heat.

Meanwhile, in a large skillet, heat the olive oil and garlic over medium-low heat and cook until the garlic starts sizzling with little bubbles around it. Add the basil and sizzle in the oil until it releases its sweet aroma, about 15 seconds. Add the tomatoes, season with a heavy pinch of salt, and cook until the bubbling tomatoes have lost their raw flavor but still taste bright and tangy, about 10 minutes.

Once the water has reached a rolling boil, season with salt until it tastes like a seasoned soup. Working in batches so the gnocchi have plenty of room to move around, drop in the gnocchi and cook just until they float and are tender, 2 to 2½ minutes. Transfer the gnocchi to the pan with the sauce, or to a separate baking dish along with the sauce.

recipe continues

Scatter the mozzarella pieces over the gnocchi, then toss gently in the pan until the gnocchi, cheese, and sauce are mixed. Sprinkle the Parmigiano-Reggiano evenly over the top.

Bake until the mozzarella is melted and a light-brown Parmigiano-Reggiano crust begins to form, 5 to 10 minutes.

Garnish with whole basil leaves and serve immediately.

GORGEOUS TIPS

I bake gnocchi alla sorrentina directly in the same ovenproof skillet I use on the stove for the tomato sauce—I use copper, but cast iron or stainless steel both work brilliantly. If you don't have an ovenproof pan, once the gnocchi have finished cooking, simply transfer them to a baking dish with the sauce before putting them in the oven. You can also just finish cooking the gnocchi in the pan and melt the cheese on the stovetop—skipping the baking step—but you won't get the same caramelized cheese crust.

Turn gnocchi alla sorrentina into *all'arrabbiata*, a spicy version of the dish, by adding slivers of fresh chilies to the tomato sauce or by adding chili flakes before you bake the pasta.

If you are using very fresh mozzarella and it is watery, before mixing it into the sauce, place the torn pieces in a colander to drain and pat dry with paper towels to eliminate the excess liquid. This will help you create the perfect cheese melt.

CRUSHING TOMATOES BY HAND

When a recipe calls for canned whole peeled tomatoes, more often than not, I ask that you crush them by hand. This is such a soothing and therapeutic process for me, as I love being in direct contact with the gorgeous ingredient. Pour the tomatoes out of the can into a medium bowl, then tenderly squeeze them between your fingers until they begin to disappear into the sauce. A little bit of splatter is inevitable—tomatoes are juicy by nature! Resist the desire to use an immersion blender to break up the tomatoes instead of doing it by hand. Hand-crushing tomatoes is a gentler approach that preserves the tomatoes' structure. Blending also splits the seeds, which will release a bitter flavor into the sauce.

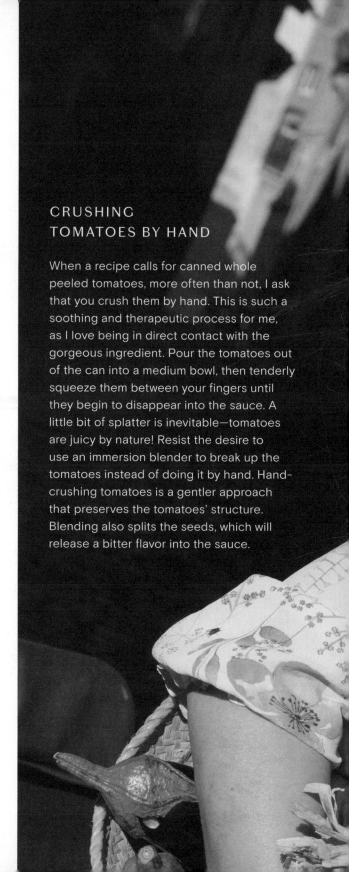

PASTA E FAGIOLI *con* PASTA MISTA CORTA

PASTA WITH BEANS AND
MIXED SHORT PASTA

Serves 4

———

Total prep and cooking time:
9½ hours
(including bean soaking time)

———

Alternate pasta shapes:
ditali, maltagliati

¾ pound dried borlotti or cannellini,
or beans of your choice, soaked
overnight and drained

3 tablespoons extra-virgin olive oil,
plus more for drizzling

1 medium white onion, diced

1 celery stalk

1 carrot

Sea salt

115 grams/4 ounces cherry or
grape tomatoes, or canned whole
peeled tomatoes, crushed by hand
(see page 58)

1 Parmigiano-Reggiano rind
(optional)

9 ounces pasta mista corta

Freshly ground black pepper

Parmigiano-Reggiano, for dusting

Fresh rosemary sprigs

I have learned many of life's most beautiful lessons over a bowl of pasta e fagioli. The most precious of these was told to me by my Aunt Stella: The secret to longevity is to cook your own meals, not to take life too seriously, and always try to be calm in the face of difficulties, even in the most stressful of situations. Stella and her sisters, Maria and Sandra, are in their eighties now and have always cooked everything from scratch using their own homemade ingredients. They eat meat very rarely, only on holidays and Sundays, so vegetables are a staple—especially beans. One of their favorite dishes has always been a seasoned soup of beans simmered with *pasta mista* (scraps of pasta; these days pasta companies from around Naples sell boxed versions of it). My aunts would gather bits of leftover pasta from the pantry and stir it into a delicious pot of beans, treating the scraps as though they were the finest designer pasta. Whenever I make this simple soup, I always think of my aunts, their lessons, and how their mostly plant-based diet was always nourishing, heartwarming, and bursting with flavor. Even in difficult times, they've taught me that life, just like pasta e fagioli, can always be delicious.

In a medium pot, combine the beans and enough water to cover—I aim for about 2 inches. Do not salt the water—it will make the beans tough. Bring to a boil over high heat, then reduce the heat to low, cover, and simmer for 1 hour.

Meanwhile, in a large pot, heat the olive oil, onion, celery, carrot, and a heavy pinch of salt over low heat. Cook until the vegetables are soft and just beginning to caramelize, about 15 minutes. Add the tomatoes and cook until they lose their raw flavor, about 5 minutes.

Add the beans and a bit of their cooking water to the large pot along with the Parmigiano-Reggiano rind (if using). Simmer over low heat until the beans are tender, about 1 hour.

Remove the celery and carrot and discard. Add the pasta directly to the pot of beans and cook until al dente. Taste frequently to determine when the pasta is done. If necessary, add very hot water a quarter cup at a time, to keep the pasta submerged and to keep the bean soup loose and chowder-like. Season with salt to taste.

Serve topped with a scrunch of pepper, a drizzle of olive oil, a dusting of Parmigiano-Reggiano, and a rosemary sprig.

GORGEOUS TIPS

You can use jarred or canned beans if you like, as long as they have already been boiled to tenderness.

To soak the beans, place them in a large container with three times their volume of water and place them, uncovered, in the refrigerator. After the beans have soaked for at least 8 hours (or overnight), drain them and set them aside until you're ready to start cooking.

Once the beans are tender and before you add the pasta, you can remove half of the beans from the pot—careful, they are hot!—and blend them with an immersion blender or in a food processor to create a smooth bean puree, then return them to the pot. This will give you a creamier consistency, versus the thicker, stew-like texture if you don't blend. Either way, it's up to you!

Have a small pot of boiling water ready next to your pot of beans when you add the pasta. If the pasta needs a bit more liquid to finish cooking, you can add the hot water ¼ cup at a time.

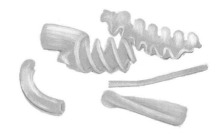

TAGLIATELLE *al* RAGÙ *di* LADY CATERINA

FRESH PASTA
WITH MY GRANDMOTHER'S
MEAT RAGÙ

Serves 4

———

Total prep and cooking time:
2 hours 15 minutes
(includes making the ragù)

———

Alternate pasta shapes:
fresh fettuccine, fresh pappardelle

6 cups Ragù di Lady Caterina
(page 64)

1 pound fresh tagliatelle,
homemade (see page 9)
or store-bought

60 grams/3 ounces (about ¾ cup)
finely grated Parmigiano-Reggiano,
plus more for dusting

———

WATCH THIS RECIPE

Ragù can be any meat or fish sauce that simmers for a long time to make its ingredients tender and almost melt together. Italy's most famous is ragù alla bolognese, named after the city of its birth. My version, which is named after its creator, my nonna, was invented far from Bologna, so it's a little different. It is a savory union of sausage and beef, to which she added mushrooms and peas at the request of my Nonno Agostino. We devoured it every Sunday, dripping it over golden nests of tagliatelle, or, on special occasions, layering it between sheets of Sfoglia all'Uovo (page 9) to make Lasagna al Ragù di Lady Caterina (page 71). For me, this recipe is the perfect Sunday dish. I like to take my time with it, invite my children to help knead and roll the pasta, and sit around the stove as the sauce bubbles, creating Lady Caterina ragù memories around my own family table.

Make the ragù as directed.

Meanwhile, bring a large pot of water to a rolling boil.

If making the fresh tagliatelle, prepare the dough as directed in the recipe. Do this next to your stove: The sauce and the pasta need to breathe the same air in order to fully become one.

Once the water is at a rolling boil, season with salt until the water tastes like a seasoned soup. Drop in the tagliatelle and cook until tender, 2 to 3 minutes.

Add the pasta to the ragù along with a ladle (½ cup) of the tears of the gods. Serve a tangle of tagliatelle, spooning over any luscious ragù left behind in the pan, and dust it with a waterfall of Parmigiano-Reggiano.

recipe continues

GORGEOUS TIP

I always make way more ragù than I need, doubling or even tripling the recipe. It freezes well, so I love to make a big batch on Sunday and use the leftovers throughout the week.

Ragù di Lady Caterina

Makes about 10 cups

---

3 tablespoons extra-virgin olive oil

1 medium white onion, diced

2 carrots, peeled and diced

2 celery stalks, diced

Sea salt

1 cup fresh or frozen peas

1 (8-ounce) sweet Italian sausage link

1½ pounds ground beef (85% lean)

½ pound mushrooms (I like button or cremini), diced

¾ cup dry white wine

1 tablespoon finely chopped fresh parsley

3 pounds whole peeled tomatoes

In a large deep sauté pan, heat the olive oil, onion, carrot, and celery over low heat. Season with salt and cook until soft and tender, about 15 minutes.

Add the peas, then use your hands to squeeze the sausage out of its casing, raining bits of sausage into the pan. Increase the heat to medium and cook the sausage, breaking it into small pieces as it cooks, until it is just kissed by the heat and begins to brown, about 3 minutes.

Add the beef and mushrooms and season once again with salt—an essential ritual for building complex flavors in Caterina's ragù. Once the beef begins to brown and release its juices, add the wine and simmer until the alcohol aroma dissipates and the liquid is reduced by about half, about 1½ minutes. Sprinkle in the parsley, then add the tomatoes, pressing them into the meat with the back of a wooden spoon or with a potato masher until they are incorporated into the meat sauce. Reduce the heat to low, cover, and simmer for 1½ hours.

I recommend making a large batch of this long-simmered sauce and freezing what you don't need for your recipe to use another time.

RIGATONI *alla* PAPALINA

🍂

THE POPE'S RIGATONI

Serves 4

———

Total prep and cooking time:
35 minutes

———

Alternate pasta shapes:
mezze maniche, fresh fettuccine

¼ cup extra-virgin olive oil

1 small white onion, diced

Sea salt

7 ounces mushrooms
(I like cremini or button), sliced

Freshly ground black pepper

¾ cup fresh or frozen peas
(if using fresh, cook in salted water
until tender, about 2 minutes)

6 slices (about 5 ounces)
thinly sliced Prosciutto di Parma,
torn into 1-inch pieces

1 cup heavy cream

½ cup tomato puree

1 pound rigatoni

30 grams/1 ounce (¼ cup plus
2 tablespoons) finely grated
Parmigiano-Reggiano, plus more for
dusting

Growing up in the shadow of the Vatican means the Pope is never far away: both literally in that he is greeting pilgrims in St. Peter's Square every Wednesday and Sunday, and figuratively in that neighborhood businesses use his name and likeness. One of my favorite places that does this is Osteria Dei Pontefici (The Pope's Tavern) located on Via Gregorio VII, a wide avenue also named for a pope. Sticking with this theme, Dei Pontefici serves *rigatoni alla papalina*, a pasta dish named for the head of the Catholic church. Legend has it that in the late 1950s carbonara was becoming popular in Rome, but it was looked down upon by Pope Pius XII as a rustic and vulgar dish. He commanded his cook to make him something lighter and more elegant, and the cook landed on a gorgeous blend of mushrooms, peas, prosciutto, cream, and tomatoes. I don't totally agree with Pope Pius XII's chef that this is a light dish—it's very rich and decadent, just like the pope himself—but it is undeniably delicious, and one bite of it always transports me home.

Bring a large pot of water to a rolling boil over high heat.

In a large deep sauté pan, heat the olive oil, onion, and a heavy pinch of salt over medium-low heat until the onion becomes slightly translucent and release all of its flavor into the olive oil, 3 to 4 minutes. Add the mushrooms and season with salt and a scrunch of pepper. Cook until the mushrooms are soft, about 5 minutes.

Add the peas, prosciutto, and a ladle (½ cup) of the boiling salty water. Increase the heat to medium and let them cook together for about a minute to infuse their flavors. Add the heavy cream, tomato puree, and a pinch of salt and simmer, stirring frequently, until the sauce thickens, about 5 minutes.

Once the water has reached a rolling boil, season with salt until the water tastes like a seasoned soup. Drop in the pasta and cook until very al dente (a little more than half the recommended cooking time).

Transfer the pasta to the sauté pan along with a ladle (½ cup) of pasta water, increase the heat to medium-high, and cook until al dente, adding more water as needed to cook the pasta and keep the sauce luscious. Remove from the heat and stir in the Parmigiano-Reggiano.

Serve dusted with more Parmigiano-Reggiano.

SPAGHETTONI *alla* PUTTANESCA

THICK SPAGHETTI
WITH TOMATO, OLIVES,
CAPERS, AND SALTED
ANCHOVIES

Serves 4

Total prep and cooking time:
25 minutes

Alternate pasta shapes:
spaghetti, linguine

¼ cup extra-virgin olive oil

4 salt-packed anchovy fillets, rinsed

1 small white onion, diced

1 garlic clove, diced

1 tablespoon roughly chopped
fresh parsley leaves, plus more for
garnish

Sea salt

2 tablespoons capers
(rinsed and soaked if salt-packed,
drained if in brine)

½ cup pitted small olives (I like
Gaeta and Kalamata)

1 cup dry white wine

1 (28-ounce) can whole peeled
tomatoes, crushed by hand
(see page 58)

1 pound spaghettoni

The myth surrounding this Neapolitan classic suggests that it was created by *puttane* (ladies of the night) who would whip up a powerful pasta dish for their lovers. It's a great story but likely untrue. I like to think of puttanesca as more of a *puttanata* (a "mess") made by throwing together pantry scraps that you might find in a typical Neapolitan kitchen. Regardless of its origins, this dish is one of my all-time top favorite pastas because it employs powerfully flavored salted anchovies, capers, and olives, turning it into something so beautiful (just like you are) that you just can't ignore it. The tomato is the lover's embrace that binds the flavors together and provides a stage for the aromas of the other ingredients, all of which mingle with the *spaghettoni* (extra-thick spaghetti) strands.

Bring a large pot of water to a rolling boil over high heat.

In a large deep sauté pan, heat the olive oil, anchovies, onion, garlic, parsley, and a heavy pinch of salt over medium-low heat. Cook until the onion becomes slightly translucent and releases all of its flavor into the olive oil, 3 to 4 minutes. Add the capers, olives, and wine. Increase the heat to medium-high and cook until the alcohol aroma evaporates and the liquid reduces by half, about 1½ minutes. Add the tomatoes, season with salt, and simmer vigorously until the tomatoes lose their raw flavor, about 8 minutes.

Once the water has reached a rolling boil, season with salt until it tastes like a seasoned soup. Drop in the pasta and cook until very al dente (a little more than half the recommended cooking time).

Transfer the pasta to the sauté pan along with a ladle (½ cup) of pasta cooking water and cook the pasta in the sauce until the pasta is al dente. Check frequently to see when the pasta is done and add more pasta cooking water as needed to finish cooking the pasta while keeping the sauce juicy.

Serve with parsley sprinkled on top.

I use salt-packed capers, rinsing them and then soaking them in several changes of water until they are pleasantly salty, but not excessively so. If you can't find salted capers, you can use good-quality ones packed in brine or high-quality extra-virgin olive oil. No need to rinse and soak the capers in that case.

Variations

PUTTANESCA ANGELA'S WAY:

My stepmother, Angela, makes my absolute favorite twist on this dish, adding canned tuna instead of salted anchovies. To make puttanesca in Angela's style, omit the anchovies and instead add two 5-ounce cans of tuna (I like yellowfin) in olive oil. Drain off the oil, flake the tuna, and add it after the white wine has evaporated. Spoon some the tears of the gods over the tuna to soften it before adding the tomato.

A VERY FANCY PUTTANESCA:

For a very special puttanesca variation, I use tinned ventresca di tonno *(cured tuna belly), a luscious and rich product from Sicily and Sardinia. It has such an exceptional flavor that I leave out the tomato altogether, which would overpower the fatty yet delicate tuna belly.*

LASAGNA *al* RAGÙ *di* LADY CATERINA

PASTA SHEETS LAYERED
WITH RAGÙ AND BÉCHAMEL

Makes 1 tray measuring
9 × 13 inches (4 to 6 servings)

Total prep and cooking time:
2¼ hours

Alternate pasta shape:
sfoglia verde

6 cups Ragù di Lady Caterina
(page 64)

1 pound fresh mozzarella, torn into
1-inch pieces

1½ cups Béchamel (page 72)

250 grams/9 ounces (about 3 cups)
finely grated Parmigiano-Reggiano

Sfoglia all'Uovo (page 9) or about
1 pound store-bought fresh pasta
sheets

GORGEOUS TIP

There is absolutely no shame in
buying premade pasta sheets or
lasagna noodles for this recipe.
Just follow the directions on the
package for preparation before
layering in the pan.

Lunch at my Nonna Caterina's was an all-day affair. Plates
would start to hit the table around noon: plump and juicy
buffalo mozzarella balls sliced into wedges to be greedily
devoured; platters of fried peppers and eggplants; pan-wilted
escarole spiked with salted anchovies, garlic, pine nuts, and
raisins; heaps of lettuce just plucked from the garden served
with olive oil and lemon, and so much more. Pasta Bro—my
brother, Agostino—and I would hover around the table until
all the guests arrived around 2 p.m., sneaking bites when no
one was watching.

The whole spread could have been a meal on its own,
but those were just the antipasti before the next course of
lasagna—pasta sheets layered with my nonna's signature ragù
and béchamel and baked in trays until the edges twisted and
crisped. Nonna Caterina always said her lasagna was a bit
rebellious—only three or four layers of pasta versus what she
said was the standard five or six. She always found the time and
energy to do it all, and now so do I, gathering my family around
the table every Sunday just as she did.

Preheat the oven to 375°F.

Spoon ½ cup ragù on the bottom of a 9 × 13-inch baking dish.
Make layers in this order: Pasta or pasta strips (there's no
need to cook the pasta in advance; it will cook in the juices of
the ragù), ½ cup ragù, one-quarter of the mozzarella,
½ cup béchamel, and ½ cup Parmigiano-Reggiano. Repeat
this layering two more times (for a total of 3 layers), cover
with a final sheet of pasta, and layer with the remaining ragù,
mozzarella, béchamel, and Parmigiano-Reggiano.

Cover the baking dish with foil and bake for 40 minutes.
Uncover and continue baking until the edges of the pasta are
curled up and browned, 20 to 30 minutes longer. Allow the
lasagna to rest for about 30 minutes before serving in slices.

recipe continues

Béchamel

Béchamel is the glue that holds lasagna together, and it makes a fantastic base for cheesy pasta bakes. When it cools it becomes hard to spread, so either make it just as you are beginning to assemble your pasta or make it in advance and reheat it as you start.

Makes about 2½ cups

2½ cups whole milk

4 tablespoons (½ stick) unsalted butter

¼ cup all-purpose flour

A pinch of freshly grated nutmeg

Sea salt

In a small saucepan, heat the milk over medium-low heat.

In a separate small saucepan, melt the butter over medium heat until frothy. Whisk in the flour with the passion of an Italian until the mixture is lightly browned and smells nutty, about 3 minutes. Add the warmed milk and continue whisking until the mixture thickens enough to coat the back of a spoon, about 3 minutes longer. Season with the nutmeg and salt to taste.

TIMBALLO *di* PASTA E POLPETTINE

PASTA BAKED WITH
MEATBALLS

Serves 4

———

Total prep and cooking time:
1 hour 15 minutes

———

Alternate pasta shapes:
anelletti, candele spezzate, ziti lunghi

Sea salt

1 pound ziti

Polpettine (page 76)

1 (28-ounce) can whole peeled
tomatoes, crushed by hand
(see page 58)

4 to 6 fresh basil leaves, torn

6 thin slices (about 4 ounces)
provolone

100 grams/3½ ounces
(about 1½ cups) finely grated
Parmigiano-Reggiano

Nonna Caterina didn't always have hours to pull together a lasagna (see Lasagna al Ragù di Lady Caterina, page 71), but she never cut corners on deliciousness. One of her go-to weekday dishes was pasta baked with meatballs bound together with melted cheese. There's a big controversy in Italy about pasta and meatballs. It's not typical in most of its fiercely regional cuisines so many Italians write it off as a purely American invention. After all, spaghetti (a first course) and meatballs (a second course) are traditionally served separately. Still, I know for a fact that many families, including mine, have gone against the grain and served pasta *with* meatballs for generations. All over the south of Italy and in parts of Abruzzo, *nonne* bake trays of pasta studded with tiny meatballs, proving that the combination does indeed exist!

Preheat the oven to 400°F.

Bring a large pot of water to a rolling boil over high heat. Season with salt until the water tastes like a seasoned soup. Drop in the pasta and cook until very al dente (a little more than half the recommended cooking time).

Meanwhile, in a large ovenproof skillet, combine the browned polpettine and tomatoes. Bring to a simmer over medium heat and simmer for 10 minutes to marry the flavors and take the raw flavor out of the tomatoes. Add the basil and simmer for 1 minute more.

Fold the pasta into the pan, distribute the provolone and Parmigiano-Reggiano evenly over the pasta. Cover with foil and bake for 15 minutes. Uncover and bake until a crisp crust forms around the edge of the dish, about 10 minutes longer.

Allow the timballo to set for 5 minutes before slicing and serving.

recipe continues

Polpettine

SMALL MEATBALLS

These tiny meatballs are tender and delicious thanks to using the soft interior of day-old bread soaked in milk or even leftover liquid from Homemade Ricotta (page 186). You can use water, too. This technique makes much moister meatballs than you get with dried bread crumbs. To make your own bread crumbs from day-old bread, cut off the crusts and shred the interior by hand into the smallest pieces possible, ideally the size of coffee grounds, or use a food processor.

Makes about 50 polpettine

———

¼ cup plus 2 tablespoons fresh bread crumbs or fine dried bread crumbs

¼ cup milk

8 ounces ground beef (85% lean)

4 ounces ground pork

60 grams/2 ounces (about ¾ cup) finely grated Parmigiano-Reggiano

1 garlic clove, minced

1 small egg

2 teaspoons sea salt

½ teaspoon roughly chopped fresh parsley leaves

Freshly ground black pepper

3 tablespoons extra-virgin olive oil

Soak the fresh bread crumbs in the milk for a couple of minutes. (If using dried bread crumbs, do not soak.) Drain off any liquid.

In a large bowl, massage together the beef, pork, bread crumbs, Parmigiano-Reggiano, garlic, egg, salt, parsley, and a scrunch of pepper. Form the mixture into balls about the size of an acorn and set aside on a baking sheet.

In a large skillet, heat the oil over medium-high heat until it shimmers. Add the meatballs and brown all over, about 7 minutes. Remove from the heat and set aside.

PASTA *con* LE PATATE

CREAMY POTATOES WITH
PASTA

Serves 4

———

Total prep and cooking time:
55 minutes

———

Alternate pasta shapes:
conchiglie, mista corta

¼ cup extra-virgin olive oil

½ medium white onion, roughly
chopped

Sea salt

1½ pounds (about 6 medium)
potatoes (I like Yukon Gold or any
yellow-fleshed potato), peeled and
cut into 1-inch pieces

Freshly ground black pepper

1 pound ditalini

100 grams/3½ ounces
(about 1½ cups) finely grated
Pecorino Romano

50 grams/1¾ ounces (about ½ cup
plus 2 tablespoons) coarsely grated
provolone (I like smoked provolone)

———

WATCH THIS RECIPE

Potatoes are everywhere in southern Italian recipes: folded into pasta dough, bread dough, and even cookie dough. My family used them almost daily, and pasta con le patate made by my Zia Stella is still one of the best things I have ever tasted. Pasta Bro and I always did our part to help source the ingredients. My nonno would ride his tractor over the volcanic soil of his potato crop and we would follow close behind, collecting the potatoes loosened from the dirt to bring them to Zia Pina's kitchen. She would transform them into pure comfort food.

This flavorful potato soup is particularly special because the pasta cooks directly in the pot with the potatoes, a technique called *pasta minestrata*, so it releases all of its wonderful starch and mingles with that of the potatoes to create the ultimate creaminess. I prefer to use water for cooking the potatoes and pasta because I like the delicate flavor, but if you want something stronger you can use store-bought or Homemade Vegetable Broth (page 115) or Homemade Chicken Stock (page 139) instead.

In a medium pot, bring 8 cups water to a rolling boil over medium-high heat.

Meanwhile, in a separate large pot, heat the olive oil, onion, and a heavy pinch of salt over medium-low heat and cook until the onion becomes slightly translucent and release all of its flavors into the olive oil, 3 to 4 minutes.

Add the potatoes to the pot with the onion, season with salt once again, add a scrunch of pepper, and cover with enough of the boiling water to completely cover the potatoes. Increase the heat to medium, cover, and cook until the potatoes are soft and tender, about 25 minutes, adding more boiling water as needed to keep the potatoes mostly covered.

recipe continues

Remove about half of the potatoes and set aside. In a food processor (or with an immersion blender in the pot), blend the remaining potatoes until smooth. Return the reserved diced potatoes to the pot along with 2 cups of the boiling water. Increase the heat to medium, bring to a simmer, then add the pasta. Cook until the pasta is al dente, stirring frequently and adding more liquid as needed to create a thick and slightly chunky soup and to finish cooking the pasta.

Remove from the heat and stir in the Pecorino Romano and the provolone.

Serve with a scrunch of pepper on top.

GORGEOUS TIP

I love making soups to use up leftovers in the fridge, and I will grate the ends of various cheeses and stir those into the pot along with the Pecorino Romano and provolone to create a slightly different—but no less delicious—flavor every time. Sometimes I even stir in some leftover sausage or salami diced into small pieces. Leave out the cheese altogether to make the dish completely vegan!

SARTÙ *di* RISO

THE KING'S CLOAK

*Makes one 10- to 12-inch sartù
(6 to 8 servings)*

———

*Total prep and cooking time:
1 hour 45 minutes*

———

¼ cup tomato paste

Sea salt

3 tablespoons extra-virgin olive oil

1 shallot, minced

2½ cups rice (Carnaroli or Arborio)

2 cup tomato puree

3 cups Ragù di Lady Caterina
(page 64)

1 (8-ounce) ball fresh mozzarella,
torn into ½-inch pieces with any
excess liquid squeezed out

50 grams/1¾ ounces cubed
(½-inch) provolone

Fresh basil leaves, for garnish

———

WATCH THIS RECIPE

Legend has it that, centuries ago, the wife of King Ferdinando of Naples made him this rice-clad ragù and cheese casserole as a shocking surprise. At the time, risotto was considered the food of the poor and sick, so she gave it a royal touch, stuffing it with a decadent and luscious filling: a rich and savory meat sauce studded with pieces of melted mozzarella and provolone cheese. I like to think of *sartù di riso* as a sort of party-sized *arancino* (Sicilian rice ball filled with meat sauce), but this dish is completely Neapolitan. When I was a teenager, I would go to friends' homes in Naples just to try slices of it served from huge round forms, the starch of the risotto having hardened by baking to contain the rich ragù within—a reminder that even the most common street food in Naples is as regal as the city herself.

The beauty of the King's Cloak is that the risotto can conceal any filling you wish. When I would travel to Naples to taste this royal delicacy, the filling would sometimes contain bits of chopped salami or cubed ham, or even a crumbled hard-boiled egg. You can fill yours with any ingredient you love to make it your own. I sometimes fold in chopped leftover broccoli rabe or sautéed kale for a pleasantly bitter kick.

Preheat the oven to 350°F.

Fill a pot with 5 cups water. Stir in the tomato paste until it dissolves to create a tomato broth. If necessary, season it with salt until it tastes like a seasoned soup and keep it warm over a very low heat as you prepare the risotto.

In a separate pot, heat the olive oil and shallot over medium-low heat. Season with salt and cook until the shallots have softened, 3 to 4 minutes. Pour in the rice and stir to coat in the oil. Continue stirring until the rice is lightly toasted and turns translucent, a couple of minutes. Add the tomato puree and cook, stirring constantly, until it has been absorbed, about

5 minutes. Add 1 cup of the prepared tomato broth and cook, stirring constantly to prevent the rice from sticking to the pan, until the broth has been absorbed, a few minutes. The rice should still be undercooked and a bit crunchy at this point, as you will finish baking it in the oven. Let the rice cool and stick together.

Line a 3-inch-deep 10- to 12-inch round baking dish with parchment paper. Using a spoon or spatula, spread three-quarters of the rice along the bottom and up the sides of the dish to make a sort of rice pie crust. Spoon the ragù evenly over the center, leveling it with a spoon, then distribute the mozzarella and provolone evenly over the ragù. Finish with a level layer of the remaining rice.

Bake until the rice is fully cooked and the cheese is melted, about 1 hour.

Allow the sartù to set for 20 minutes before plating. Invert a serving plate over the sartù pan. Flip the plate and pan over, inverting the sartù onto the plate. Serve, sliced into wedges and garnished with fresh basil leaves.

GORGEOUS TIP

If you don't have parchment paper, heavily butter the pan. The parchment paper prevents a crispy crust from forming, while a buttered *sartù* will develop a crispy outer shell. Either version is just gorgeous.

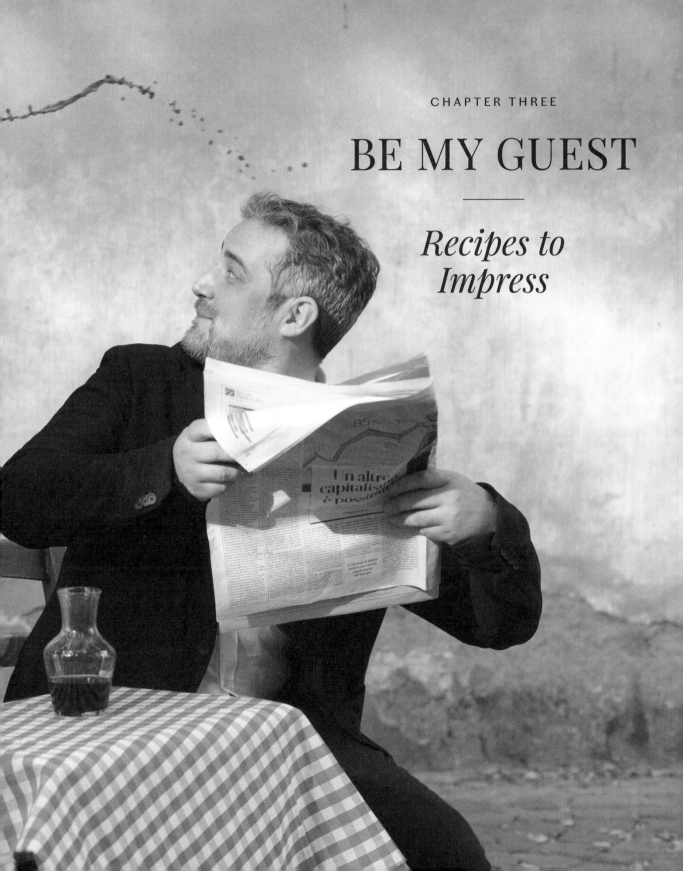

CHAPTER THREE

BE MY GUEST

—

Recipes to Impress

After high school, at the not-so-innocent age of eighteen, I decided to leave Rome for London.

I had been given an opportunity to study and join the British music industry. Even though my English was weak, my dreams for a new adventure were still superior to any doubts trying to hold me back.

Excited, I went to tell my grandfather of my plans. His side of the family was strong in tradition. Only a couple of them had traveled outside of Italy, and they had all they needed to be happy at home. So even though my grandfather had always been the most approachable for deeper conversations, I didn't know what to expect—maybe a speech about family sticking together or, at worst, being told I'd be an outcast if I left. He let me talk and never interrupted. Desperate and fumbling, I tried to explain all the reasons I should go to London with no money, very few concrete plans, and no English skills. When I was done, his kind eyes sparkled and he looked at me with a gentle, proud smile.

He said, "Go . . . just go."

And so I went. There's an interesting thing that happens when you move to a new country: Your culture becomes your medium of expression, especially when you don't speak the language. You stand out, you constantly get asked where you are from, and people inquire if you like spaghetti and pizza a lot. But it was during this experience that I realized great food can bring anyone together. It transcends language, merges cultures, and is the universal sauce for building good relationships.

I learned to understand the mindset behind a thick, creamy chicken Alfredo served in the greasy spoon of English-Italian fusion dives. The weather in my new home was cold and dreary, and heavy sauces and an overload of protein were apparently required to substitute for the lack of sun. Despite not having the best foundation to work with, I knew I could transform dishes like this into ones that reminded me of home, connecting my new friends with the simple, fresh food I had grown up with and that made me who I am. It was as if the United Kingdom welcomed me with open arms to bring passion, entertainment, and, of course, great Italian food to its people.

And I loved every moment of it.

From England to Ireland, and up to Scotland, the next few years became a blur of events, dinners, and great times with friends and colleagues. I navigated the underground jazz scene, set up concerts and festivals, and promoted music on live radio.

Everywhere I went, I would encourage my friends to try something new. Rainy and gloomy today? Try this classic penne all'arrabbiata to get your blood pumping hot! You like creamy carbonara with bacon? How about we run to the local market for some guanciale, and I'll show you how to make cream with egg and cheese. I was living in a

different universe, with people who were fascinated by the magic that happens when you produce simple dishes with a sprinkle of love.

It was around this time I found my future husband, Brook, a British bloke who had studied in the United States. By some serendipitous timing, we crossed paths. Soon I was cooking for him more than anyone else (after all, food is the ultimate language of love).

When you are preparing a meal for friends or loved ones, you will find that you naturally take more care. Every ingredient is thoroughly inspected, because it must bring about the most impressive results. The stale Parmigiano in the fridge is never selected for such occasions. Instead, the best wine for the night is picked and only the best ingredients are used. This level of care, which goes into every ingredient, every stir, and every garnish, became known to me as "passion cooking."

Through my adventures, the recipes I made were simple, built on the classics of my youth in Italy, but they were filled with love and romance and a whole lot of passion. Nowadays, I make these dishes to impress and pamper my friends, my family, and even myself when I have a rare moment alone. Each and every one of them is proof that all you need is love—and a little pasta magic—to show your nearest and dearest how much you care. That's the secret to *real* gorgeousness.

RISOTTO *alla* CREMA *di* SCAMPI

CREAMY RISOTTO WITH
LANGOUSTINES

Serves 4

---

*Total prep and cooking time:
1 hour 10 minutes*

2 pounds heads-on langoustines

3 tablespoons extra-virgin olive oil

1 shallot, minced

Sea salt

½ cup canned whole peeled
tomatoes, crushed by hand, or
tomato puree

1 cup heavy cream

2 cups rice (Carnaroli or Arborio)

1 cup dry white wine

Homemade Shellfish Stock
(page 89) or 5 cups store-bought
seafood stock or Vegetable Broth
(page 115), warmed

Roughly chopped fresh parsley
leaves, for garnish

GORGEOUS TIP

Once you've cleaned and
trimmed the langoustines,
start making the shellfish stock
and have it working while you
prepare the langoustine cream
for the risotto.

I like to think that my *risotto alla crema di scampi* was what
convinced my husband that I was going to be his wife for life.
For me, risotto, a creamy rice dish that takes patience and love
to make, is the ultimate romantic gesture. Risotto alla crema
di scampi is the most romantic risotto of all. In Italy, scampi
are langoustines, not shrimp as they are in Italian-American
shrimp scampi recipes. These pretty pink crustaceans look like
dainty little lobsters. Their meat is creamy, sweet, and delicate,
but it can easily become tough and chalky from overcooking.
Take care to cook the scampi gently, kissing them tenderly
with the heat of your stove so they can express their perfect
flavor. If you cannot find langoustines, you can substitute any
small, sweet variety of uncooked shrimp. Before using them,
peel and devein them (see How to Devein Shrimp, page 148).

Set aside 2 langoustines per person. You will cook these
whole later. Separate the bodies and tails of the remaining
langoustines: Hold the body and tail with your index fingers
and thumbs close to where the body and tail meet, then
twist in opposite directions. Set aside the bodies for making
the shellfish stock. Peel the tails by carefully breaking the
segments on the underside of the tail. The tail meat will
slip out. Chop the tail meat into small pieces and set aside.
Reserve the tail shells for making the shellfish stock.

In a medium pot, heat 1 tablespoon of the olive oil and the
shallot over medium-low heat. Season with a pinch of salt and
cook until bubbles appear around the shallot, 1 to 2 minutes.
Increase the heat to medium-high, add the tomatoes, and
cook just until they begin to reduce, 2 to 3 minutes. Add the
cream and simmer until it begins to thicken, about 3 minutes
longer. Stir in the langoustine meat and simmer for 2 to 3
minutes. Remove from the heat and blend half of the mixture
in a food processor or with an immersion blender until smooth.
Set the langoustine cream aside.

recipe continues

In a large saucepan, heat the remaining 2 table-spoons olive oil over medium-high heat until shimmering. Pour in the rice and stir to coat in the oil. Continue stirring until the rice is lightly toasted and turns translucent, a couple of minutes. Add the wine and stir until the alcohol aroma dissipates and the liquid reduces by half, about 1½ minutes. Add the langoustine cream, stirring until it is absorbed, then add enough stock to cover the rice. Cook, stirring constantly to release the starches and to keep the rice from sticking to the pan, until the stock has been absorbed, about 2 minutes. Add ½ cup of stock, stirring constantly, and wait until it has been absorbed before adding another ½ cup. Repeat until the rice is very al dente, then lay the reserved whole langoustines on top of the risotto. Cook gently over low heat until the langoustines are just cooked through (break open a tail of a langoustine, and when it is just opaque and firm, it is cooked), 3 to 4 minutes. Add more stock as necessary to finish cooking the rice and the langoustines (you may not need all the stock).

Serve immediately with the whole langoustines draped over the risotto and parsley sprinkled on top.

HOW TO EAT COOKED LANGOUSTINES

The whole langoustines in this dish aren't just a garnish: You eat them! To get to the meat, use a fork and knife to separate the body from the tail. Break the segments of the tail's underside to get at the tail meat. You can suck the heads as you would crawfish and twist off and suck on the claws for tiny bits of sweet meat.

Homemade Shellfish Stock

Makes about 5 cups

—

2 tablespoons extra-virgin olive oil

1 carrot, cut into 2-inch pieces

1 celery stalk, cut into 2-inch pieces

½ medium white onion, roughly chopped

Sea salt

Langoustine or shrimp heads and shells (trimmed from
2 pounds heads-on langoustines or shrimp)

Freshly ground black pepper

In a large pot, heat the oil over medium-low heat. Add
the carrot, celery, onion, and a heavy pinch of salt. Cook
for a few minutes, then increase the heat to medium-high
and add the shellfish heads and shells and cook briefly.
Add 1½ quarts (6 cups) water and bring to a boil, then
reduce the heat to maintain a gentle simmer and cook,
uncovered, for 20 minutes. Strain the stock, pressing all
the juice from the heads. Discard the solids.

GORGEOUS TIP

When I have a bit of black truffle on hand, I add ½ ounce in a flurry of thin slices. In that case, I omit the Parmigiano-Reggiano, which would cover the wonderfully seductive truffle aromas that deserve to take center stage.

FUSILLATA CASARECCIA
ai FUNGHI

MIXED MUSHROOM
CREAMY DELIGHT

Serves 4

Total prep and cooking time:
30 minutes

Alternate pasta shapes:
fresine, ziti, penne

2 tablespoons extra-virgin olive oil

2 tablespoons unsalted butter

1 small white onion, diced

Sea salt

1 pound fusillata casareccia

1 pound mixed wild mushrooms,
sliced or torn into bite-sized pieces

Freshly ground black pepper

2 teaspoons roughly chopped
fresh parsley leaves, plus more for
garnish

3 cups heavy cream

60 grams/2 ounces (about ¾ cup)
finely grated Parmigiano-Reggiano,
plus more for dusting

Mushrooms of one type or another are in season all year-round, but in Italy, we enjoy them most in the fall, when wild mushrooms culled from the forests pop up in market stalls. Even as a child, I loved their meaty texture and savory flavor, and I like to think of them as a meat substitute in this autumnal dish of cream sauce with mixed mushrooms served with pasta that resembles rolls of parchment. The type of mushrooms you use for this dish depends on where you are and what you love; select a variety that will bring flavor and texture contrasts to your plate. I love mixing cremini, chanterelle, button, and trumpet mushrooms.

In a large deep sauté pan, heat the olive oil, butter, onion, and a heavy pinch of salt over medium-low heat. Cook until the onion becomes slightly translucent and releases all of its flavor into the olive oil, 3 to 4 minutes.

Meanwhile, bring a large pot of water to a rolling boil over high heat. Season with salt until the water tastes like a seasoned soup. Drop in the pasta and cook until al dente.

Meanwhile, add the mushrooms and a ladle (½ cup) of pasta cooking water to the sauté pan. Season with another heavy pinch of salt and a scrunch of pepper, then sprinkle in the parsley. Increase the heat to medium-high and simmer until the mushrooms are tender, about 5 minutes. Add the cream and simmer until the sauce thickens, about 5 minutes. Remove from the heat and energetically stir in the Parmigiano-Reggiano.

Add the pasta to the pan and toss until it is coated in the thick and sultry mushroom cream sauce.

Serve sprinkled with parsley and dusted with Parmigiano-Reggiano.

CONCHIGLIE *con* PERA E GORGONZOLA

Serves 4

Total prep and cooking time:
25 minutes

Alternate pasta shapes:
conchigliette, lumache, trottole

Sea salt

1 pound conchiglie

2 tablespoons unsalted butter

2 firm pears, peeled and
coarsely grated

1 cup heavy cream

6 ounces Gorgonzola dolce

Freshly ground black pepper

¼ cup crushed walnuts, for garnish

4 Poached Pear halves
(opposite), for garnish

I like to think of this dish as the pasta version of one of my favorite things: a cheese plate. Fruit and cheese are a natural pairing on a cheese board, but we rarely think of them as partners for pasta. They are actually gorgeous together, and pear and Gorgonzola pasta is a perfect way to spice things up a bit on a weeknight. Plus, the shells of the *conchiglie* (smaller versions of the large, stuffable *conchiglioni*) are fun to eat scooped up with a big spoon, since the creamy deliciousness of the sauce gets trapped in the shells' crevices. Let pear and Gorgonzola inspire you to experiment with more fruit and cheese combinations, depending on the season. I love apple with Taleggio, berries with burrata, and figs with pecorino!

In Italy, Gorgonzola is broken down into two types: *dolce* (sweet) and *piccante* (spicy). Gorgonzola dolce isn't actually sweet, but it is more mellow than piccante, which has a fierce bite to it.

Bring a large pot of water to a rolling boil over high heat. Season with salt until it tastes like a seasoned soup. Drop in the pasta and cook until al dente.

Meanwhile, in a large deep sauté pan, melt the butter over medium heat. Add the grated pears and allow the flavors to infuse for 1 minute. Add the cream, bring to a simmer, and cook, stirring frequently, until thickened, about 5 minutes.

Add the Gorgonzola to the pan and season with salt and a scrunch of pepper. Toss in the pasta with a splash (¼ cup) of pasta cooking water. Massage it all together until the sauce thickens and the pasta is drenched in the creamy Gorgonzola sauce inside and out.

Sprinkle the pasta with the walnuts. Top each serving with half a poached pear.

Poached Pears

Makes 6 half pears

1 cup whiskey

¼ cup sugar

2 ripe pears, halved and cored

In a medium pot, heat the whiskey and ¼ cup water over high heat. Stir in the sugar and add the pears. Reduce the heat to medium-low and simmer, uncovered, until the pears are tender and can be pierced through with a fork, about 25 minutes, turning halfway through.

LINGUINE *con* COZZE, VONGOLE, E POLIPETTI

✤

LINGUINE, MUSSELS, CLAMS,
AND BABY OCTOPUS

Serves 4

———

Total prep and cooking time:
30 minutes

———

Alternate pasta shapes:
spaghetti, paccheri

½ cup extra-virgin olive oil

1 garlic clove, minced

⅓ pound baby octopus, cleaned,
or octopus, cleaned and cut into
1-inch pieces

2 pounds mussels, beards removed
and scrubbed

1½ pounds clams (I like Manila
and littleneck), rinsed (see How to
Clean Clams, page 55)

1 cup dry white wine

2 teaspoons finely chopped
fresh parsley leaves, plus more
for garnish

Sea salt

1 pound linguine

I think it's absolutely normal to fight in a relationship, and sometimes it can be hard to patch things up quickly, as neither myself nor my husband want to admit defeat. It was by chance I found out how to resolve this dilemma. After we had a big argument one day, I grabbed some fresh littlenecks, mussels, and baby octopus from the fish market. Even though I was supposed to be doing something else, I decided to take my time and spend a few hours in the kitchen cooking. Brook happened to come home early, and we didn't look at or talk to each other. All I did was serve him a plate. After he took one bite, he couldn't stop himself from smiling and he exclaimed, "This so f***ing good!" That was the end of the fight.

Whether or not you and your lover are in a fight, make this dish to blind them—or yourself!—with passion and romance.

Bring a large pot of water to a rolling boil over high heat.

Meanwhile, in a large deep sauté pan, heat the olive oil and garlic over medium-low heat and cook until the garlic starts sizzling with little bubbles around it, 1 to 2 minutes. Increase the heat to medium-high and add the baby octopus, mussels, clams, and wine. Cook, uncovered, using tongs to transfer the mussels and clams to a medium bowl as soon as they open. Some of them will open within 30 seconds, others after about 3 minutes. Discard any that do not open. Stir in the parsley and turn off the heat. Pick about three-quarters of the mussel and clam meats from their shells, discarding the shells, and set aside. Leave the remaining mussels and clams as is.

Once the water has reached a rolling boil, season with salt until the water tastes like a seasoned soup. Drop in the pasta and cook until very al dente (a little more than half the recommended cooking time).

Transfer the pasta to the sauté pan. Increase the heat to high and cook, stirring frequently, until the pasta is al dente. Check frequently to see when the pasta is done and add more pasta cooking water as needed to finish cooking the pasta and keep the sauce loose.

Just before serving the pasta, add all of the cooked mussels and clams back to the pan and toss well to warm them.

Serve with parsley sprinkled on top.

ZITI *alla* NORMA

PASTA WITH TOMATO,
FRIED EGGPLANT, AND
RICOTTA SALATA

Serves 4

Total prep and cooking time:
1 hour 35 minutes

Alternate pasta shapes:
farfalle, gemelli

4 cups cubed (½-inch) eggplant
(about 1½ large eggplants)

Sea salt

½ cup plus 3 tablespoons
extra-virgin olive oil

2 garlic cloves, minced

1 pound Roma tomatoes, seeded,
roughly chopped, and passed
through a food mill

8 fresh basil leaves, torn, plus whole
leaves for garnish

1 pound ziti

2 ounces ricotta salata, freshly
grated, for topping

My first time in Sicily was as a teenager. I spent three months on the tiny Aeolian Island of Panarea to act in a movie of the same name, and the culture shock was real. The island life was so laid-back and the opposite of Rome in so many ways. For one thing, it seemed like all of the food was fried. Still, although Sicilian dishes were often really heavy, there was one in particular I loved: *pasta alla Norma*. This incredibly summery Sicilian specialty is made by gently cooking fried bits of eggplant in a fresh tomato sauce, and the sauce's acidic tang cuts beautifully through its oil.

It is so important to use seasonal produce for this dish. Out-of-season eggplants can have an unpleasant bitterness or be flavorless. Do as they do in Panarea and make *pasta alla Norma* only when eggplants and tomatoes are at their peak summer flavor. Hit the dish with a generous flurry of ricotta salata for extra gorgeousness.

Place the eggplant in a colander and sprinkle all over with abundant salt. Set aside to drain, weighted down, for 1 hour. Rinse and pat dry with paper towels.

In a large deep sauté pan, heat ½ cup of the olive oil over medium-high heat until the oil reaches 320 to 350°F (you can either use a food thermometer or your eyes—the oil will bubble and dance around a toothpick dipped into it). Carefully add the eggplant and fry until golden brown, turning as necessary so they cook evenly, about 5 minutes per side. Drain the eggplant on paper towels.

In a large deep sauté pan, heat the remaining 3 tablespoons olive oil and the garlic over medium-low heat and cook until the garlic starts sizzling with little bubbles around it, 1 to 2 minutes. Add the tomatoes, season with salt, and cook until they break down, about 20 minutes.

recipe continues

Set aside one-quarter of the fried eggplant and stir the remaining eggplant into the sauce. Add the basil leaves and cook until the sauce begins to thicken, about 10 minutes.

Meanwhile, bring a large pot of water to a rolling boil over high heat. Season with salt until the water tastes like a seasoned soup. Drop in the pasta and cook until al dente.

Transfer the pasta to the sauté pan along with a splash (¼ cup) of pasta cooking water. Increase the heat to high and stir to coat the pasta.

Serve garnished with basil leaves, the reserved fried eggplant, and a generous flurry of ricotta salata grated on top.

HOW TO PEEL AND SEED TOMATOES

If you don't have a food mill, which will remove the skins of the tomatoes, simply blanch the tomatoes in boiling water, cutting an "X" into the butt end beforehand. Bring a pot of water to a rolling boil, then add the tomatoes and cook for 1 minute. Drain and shock in an ice bath. Remove the skins and discard them. To remove the seeds from the tomatoes, halve them lengthwise and use a spoon to scoop them out.

SPAGHETTI *alla* NERANO

SPACHETTI WITH
FRIED ZUCCHINI AND
PROVOLONE

Serves 4

———

Total prep and cooking time::
25 minutes

———

Alternate pasta shape:
spaghettoni

Sea salt

1 pound spaghetti

¼ cup plus 2 tablespoons
extra-virgin olive oil

1½ pounds (about 2 medium) small
zucchini, cut into ⅛-inch coins

1 tablespoon unsalted butter

6 to 8 fresh basil leaves, torn, plus
whole leaves for garnish

60 grams/2 ounces (about ¾ cup)
finely grated Pecorino Romano,
plus more for dusting

60 grams/2 ounces (about ¾ cup)
finely grated Provolone del Monaco
or another sharp cow's milk cheese,
plus more for dusting

Freshly ground black pepper

Legend has it that in the 1950s, a woman named Maria Grazia invented this dish of fried zucchini and cheese in her gorgeous village of Nerano near the Amalfi Coast. The recipe is simple and decadent: Fried zucchini and pasta are tossed with a sharp local cow's milk cheese called Provolone del Monaco, which is made in the Monte Lattari, the mountains above the coast. Of course the next time you visit Nerano and the Costiera, you should feast on fish. But don't neglect the soulful land-based dishes invented and beloved by locals, too. In the meantime, take yourself to Nerano with this creamy dish.

If you can't find Provolone del Monaco, use any sharp cow's milk cheese as a substitute.

Bring a large pot of water to a rolling boil over high heat. Season with salt until it tastes like a seasoned soup. Drop in the pasta and cook until very al dente (a little more than half the recommended cooking time).

Meanwhile, in a large deep sauté pan, heat the olive oil over medium heat until it shimmers. Add the zucchini, season with salt, and fry, turning once, until shiny and golden (just like you are), about 4 minutes. Remove a few coins per serving and set aside on paper towels to drain. You will use them as a garnish.

Transfer the pasta to the sauté pan along with 1 cup of pasta cooking water and stir to coat. Increase the heat to high, then fold in the butter. Toss in the torn basil leaves, stirring with passion until the pasta is al dente. Check frequently to see when the pasta is done and add more pasta cooking water as needed to finish cooking the pasta and keep the sauce loose.

Remove from the heat and stir in the Pecorino Romano and Provolone del Monaco vigorously to mantecare (see page xxii). Finish with a scrunch of pepper.

Serve garnished with the reserved zucchini coins, whole basil leaves, and a flurry of additional grated pecorino and provolone.

GORGEOUS TIP

I love adding zucchini flowers if I have them. Fry them with the zucchini coins to mix into the pasta, and set aside a few for garnish.

MEZZE MANICHE *con* GAMBERI E ZUCCHINE

Serves 4

———

*Total prep and cooking time:
35 minutes*

———

Alternate pasta shapes:
pennette, paccheri

3 tablespoons extra-virgin olive oil

1 garlic clove, minced

1 pound zucchini, cut into ¼-inch
coins

230 grams/8 ounces grape
tomatoes, halved

Sea salt and freshly ground
black pepper

1 cup dry white wine

1 pound mezze maniche

¾ pound raw shrimp, peeled and
deveined, tails left on

2 teaspoons roughly chopped
fresh parsley leaves, plus more for
garnish

Sweet red shrimp belong with pasta any time of the year, but the zucchini and cherry tomatoes in this recipe absolutely scream Italian summer: a long, hot stretch from June until late September when market stalls burst with summer squash and no fewer than ten types of tomatoes. This is a dish I would cook for Brook and our friends when I was dreaming about Italian sunshine—as you may have noticed, my time in the UK was filled with some intense moments of homesickness. But you can make this super-fast, 20-minute dish for whenever you're craving a taste of summer. For maximum flavor, use mezze maniche, a pasta shape whose name translates to "short sleeves," which is essentially half rigatoni. Each piece is ready to sneakily hide a bit of zucchini or shrimp in its ridged, tubular shape.

Bring a large pot of water to a rolling boil over high heat.

In a large deep sauté pan, heat the olive oil and garlic over medium-low heat and cook until the garlic starts sizzling with little bubbles around it, 1 to 2 minutes. Increase the heat to medium-high, add the zucchini and tomatoes, and season with salt and a scrunch of pepper. Add the wine and cook until the alcohol aroma evaporates and the liquid has reduced by half, about 1½ minutes.

Once the water has reached a rolling boil, season with salt until the water tastes like a seasoned soup. Drop in the pasta and cook until very al dente (a little more than half the recommended cooking time).

Meanwhile, continue cooking the zucchini and tomatoes until they soften, about 5 minutes. Add the shrimp and parsley.

Transfer the pasta to the sauté pan along with a splash (¼ cup) of pasta cooking water. Finish cooking the shrimp and pasta together, adding more pasta cooking water as needed until the pasta is al dente and the shrimp has turned pink.

Serve with parsley sprinkled on top.

GORGEOUS TIP

If you want to give this dish a Sardinian twist—and I sometimes do, to remind myself of lazy holidays I have spent on that gorgeous Italian island—I leave the tomato out and grate over a bit of fresh pecorino cheese before serving. The cheese lends a wonderful savory note, seasoning the shrimp and zucchini with its zesty flavor. Cheese and seafood are usually a strict no-no, but rules are always made to be broken, and leave it to the wild Sardinians to do it!

GORGEOUS TIP

To make this a vegan recipe,
leave out the cream and butter
and instead double the amount
of extra-virgin olive oil used to
sizzle the garlic.

SPAGHETTI *al* LIMONE

SPAGHETTI WITH CREAMY LEMON SAUCE

Serves 4

Total prep and cooking time:
20 minutes

Alternate pasta shapes:
spaghettini, tonnarelli

Sea salt

1 pound spaghetti

3 tablespoons unsalted butter

2 garlic cloves, minced

2 tablespoons extra-virgin olive oil

Grated zest of 2 lemons
(about 2 tablespoons), plus more
for garnish

Juice of 1 lemon (about
3 tablespoons)

2 cups heavy cream

WATCH THIS RECIPE

I can't and will never forget my first encounter with a lemon tree. My nonno had an old wooden ladder that he would use to pick fresh lemons, but I was always too scared to try to climb it. One day, however, the lemons looked so ripe and so yellow that I couldn't resist. I mustered all my courage and climbed the narrow rungs, reaching out to pick the giant lemon that was calling my name. As I ripped it from the branch, it released some divine essence that hit my senses. It was love at first smell! My lemon obsession had officially begun.

This creamy and tangy pasta dish is a luscious love letter to that first encounter. The touch of butter and splash of cream make it rich, while the citrusy tang keeps it fresh, vibrant, and juicy.

Bring a large pot of water to a rolling boil over high heat. Season with salt until the water tastes like a seasoned soup. Drop in the pasta and cook until very al dente (a little more than half the recommended cooking time).

Meanwhile, in a large deep sauté pan, heat the butter and garlic over medium-low heat and cook until the garlic starts sizzling with little bubbles around it, 1 to 2 minutes. Add the olive oil, then the lemon zest and lemon juice and let the flavors mingle. Pour in the cream and season with a heavy pinch of salt. Bring to a simmer over medium-high heat and cook, stirring frequently, until the cream sauce begins to thicken, about 5 minutes longer.

Transfer the pasta to the sauté pan along with a ladle (½ cup) of pasta cooking water. Cook the pasta until al dente. Check frequently to see when the pasta is done and add more pasta cooking water as needed to finish cooking the pasta and keep the sauce loose.

Serve with lemon zest sprinkled on top.

RISOTTO COZZE E PECORINO

RISOTTO WITH
MUSSELS AND SHEEP'S
MILK CHEESE

Serves 4

Total prep and cooking time:
35 minutes

3 cups Homemade Shellfish Stock
(see page 89) or Homemade
Vegetable Broth (page 115)

4 tablespoons extra-virgin olive oil

1 shallot, diced

Sea salt

2 cups rice (Carnaroli or Arborio)

1 cup dry white wine

1 garlic clove, minced

2 pounds mussels, beards removed
and scrubbed

2 tablespoons unsalted butter

150 grams/5¼ ounces
(about 2¾ cups) finely grated young
pecorino, plus more for dusting

Roughly chopped fresh parsley
leaves, for garnish

As I've mentioned, one of the biggest controversies in Italy is whether or not cheese and fish can be combined. There are many rules guiding the way that we Italians eat and, while we never sprinkle Parmigiano-Reggiano (or any other cheese for that matter) on top of our Spaghetti alle Vongole (page 53), we absolutely do combine cheese (especially sheep's milk varieties) and seafood together in other dishes, especially in Southern Italy. This risotto is inspired by the gorgeous and sensual cuisine of Puglia, the "heel" of the Italian boot and home to my stepmother, Angela, and her mother, Nonna Michelina, two phenomenal cooks. It is a creamy and beautifully balanced reminder that seafood and cheese can indeed be a perfect pairing, and it will take you directly to Puglia's Adriatic Coast.

In a medium saucepan, bring the stock to a boil over high heat, then reduce the heat and keep at a low simmer.

In a large skillet, heat 3 tablespoons of the oil, the shallot, and a heavy pinch of salt over low heat and cook until the shallot becomes soft, 3 to 4 minutes. Increase the heat to medium-high, pour in the rice, and stir to coat in the oil. Continue stirring until the rice is lightly toasted and turns translucent, a couple of minutes. Add the wine and stir until the alcohol aroma dissipates and the liquid reduces by half, about 1½ minutes. Add enough stock to cover the rice and cook, stirring constantly to release the starches and to keep the rice from sticking to the pan, until the stock has been absorbed, about 2 minutes. Add ½ cup of stock, stirring constantly, and wait until it has been absorbed before adding another ½ cup. Repeat until the rice is al dente. You may not need all the stock.

Meanwhile, in a large pot, heat the remaining 1 tablespoon oil over low heat. Add the garlic over medium-low heat and cook until the garlic starts sizzling with little bubbles around it, 1 to 2 minutes. Increase the heat to medium-high and add the mussels. Cook, uncovered, using tongs to transfer the mussels to a medium bowl as soon as they open. Some will open within 30 seconds, others after about 3 minutes. Discard

any that do not open. Pick about three-quarters of the mussel meats from their shells, discarding the shells, and set aside. Leave the remaining mussels as is.

Stir the butter into the rice. Remove from the heat and fold in the pecorino. Gently fold in all of the mussels and the mussel cooking juices from the pot.

Serve dusted with pecorino and parsley.

The DEVIL'S KISS

RIGATONI WITH SMOKED
TOMATO, CALABRIAN CHILI,
AND VODKA CREAM SAUCE

Serves 4

Total prep and cooking time:
30 minutes

Alternate pasta shapes:
penne, potato gnocchi

4 ounces pancetta, cut into ¼-inch
dice

1 tablespoon extra-virgin olive oil

½ small white onion, diced

1 garlic clove, minced

Sea salt

¼ cup tomato paste

1 cup vodka

1 tablespoon Calabrian chili paste

18 ounces fire-roasted
whole tomatoes or whole canned
peeled tomatoes, crushed by hand
(see page 58)

1 cup heavy cream

1 pound rigatoni

60 grams/2 ounces (about ¾ cup)
finely grated Parmigiano-Reggiano

Whole fresh chili peppers, for
garnish

This recipe is burning fire (just like you are) and satisfies all
my cravings for intense heat. Legend has it that Lucifer and his
wife, Lilith, declared their love for each other over this dish, so
it's no wonder that eating it feels like being kissed by the devil
himself. The heat comes from the chili paste, while the fire-
roasted tomatoes contribute a smoky undertone. The heat and
fire are sealed in a sacred bond with the vodka cream sauce,
which only slightly tames the devilish spice.

Bring a large pot of water to a rolling boil over high heat.

In a large deep sauté pan, sizzle the pancetta in the olive oil
over medium-low heat. Once the pancetta begins to brown
and release its fat, about 5 minutes, add the onion, garlic, and a
pinch of salt. Cook until the onion becomes slightly translucent
and releases all of its flavor into the olive oil, 3 to 4 minutes.
Add the tomato paste and increase the heat to medium, stirring
to envelop the onion and garlic in the intense paste. Fry until
the tomato paste turns a brick hue, about 2 minutes. Add the
vodka and simmer until the alcohol aroma evaporates and
the liquid has reduced by half, about 1½ minutes. Add the
Calabrian chili paste and cook until fragrant, about 15 seconds.
Pour in the tomatoes and cream, stirring passionately to
combine. Season with salt, then increase the heat to medium-
high to simmer for 5 minutes to thicken the sauce and let the
flavors perfectly mingle.

Once the water has reached a rolling boil, season with salt until
the water tastes like a seasoned soup. Drop in the pasta and
cook until al dente.

Transfer the pasta to the sauté pan along with a ladle (½ cup)
of pasta cooking water and massage together like a temptress
until the rigatoni are drenched in the spicy, silky sauce.
Remove from the heat and stir in the Parmigiano-Reggiano.

Serve garnished with chili peppers.

RISOTTO *ai* FUNGHI PORCINI

RISOTTO WITH
PORCINI MUSHROOMS

Serves 4

Total prep and cooking time:
1 hour

1 (1.7-ounce) package dried
porcini mushrooms

4 cups Homemade Vegetable Broth,
(page 115) or store-bought

3 tablespoons extra-virgin olive oil

1 small white onion, diced

Sea salt

2 cups rice (Carnaroli or Arborio)

1 cup dry white wine

2 teaspoons roughly chopped
fresh parsley leaves, plus more for
garnish

2 tablespoons unsalted butter

60 grams/2 ounces (about ¾ cup)
finely grated Parmigiano-Reggiano

Sautéed Fresh Porcini Mushrooms,
sliced (optional; page 111),
for garnish

I have been going porcini hunting with my father ever since I was a year old—I have the nostalgic Polaroids my father took as evidence. Tonino, my dad, is probably more passionate about mushrooms than anyone else I know. He's well versed in all mushroom species, especially porcini. My Riosotto ai Funghi Porcini is one of his favorite dishes, and every time I make it I think of him.

Fresh porcini are seasonal, but thankfully you can enjoy the dried version year-round! In this recipe, I combine two gorgeous ways to eat them: gently simmered in a risotto with Parmigiano-Reggiano, and sliced and sautéed to caramelized perfection as a luxurious garnish. If you can track them down, use fresh porcini for the garnish.

Soak the porcini mushrooms in lukewarm water until they plump up, about 30 minutes. Reserving the soaking liquid (which is flavorful and aromatic and will give the risotto an amazing flavor), drain the mushrooms. Rinse the mushrooms under cold water and cut into ¼-inch-wide strips. Strain the reserved soaking liquid through a coffee filter—dried porcini mushrooms can be gritty—and set aside.

In a medium saucepan, heat the vegetable broth over low heat.

In a large saucepan, heat the olive oil, onion, and a heavy pinch of salt over medium-low heat until the onion becomes slightly translucent and releases all of its flavor into the olive oil, 3 to 4 minutes. Increase the heat to medium-high, pour in the rice, and stir to coat in the oil. Continue stirring until the rice is lightly toasted and turns translucent, a couple of minutes. Add the wine and stir until the alcohol aroma dissipates and the liquid reduces by half, about 1½ minutes.

recipe continues

Add the reserved mushroom soaking liquid, the parsley, and just enough of the broth to cover the rice. Cook, stirring constantly to release the starches and to keep the rice from sticking to the pan, until the broth has been absorbed, about 2 minutes. Add ½ cup of broth, stirring constantly, and wait until it has been absorbed before adding more broth ½ cup at a time. The rice is done when it is al dente. You may not need all the broth.

Stir the butter into the rice. Remove from the heat and fold in the Parmigiano-Reggiano.

Serve garnished with slices of sautéed porcini and a flurry of parsley sprinkled on top.

Sautéed Fresh Porcini Mushrooms

Serves 4

2 tablespoons extra-virgin olive oil

2 fresh porcini mushrooms, sliced

Sea salt and freshly ground black pepper

In a skillet, heat the oil over medium-high heat. Add the porcini, season with salt and pepper, and cook until golden, turning once, 3 to 4 minutes on each side.

TAGLIOLINI *al* TARTUFO

FRESH PASTA WITH
TRUFFLES

Serves 4

———

Total prep and cooking time:
15 minutes

———

Alternate pasta shapes:
fresh tagliatelle, fresh tonnarelli,
potato gnocchi

1¼ sticks (5 ounces) unsalted butter

Sea salt

1 ounce black truffle

1 pound homemade tagliolini
(see page 9) or 1¼ pounds store-
bought fresh tagliolini

GORGEOUS TIP

A basic truffle shaver is sold
online for around $20; designer
versions can fetch $1,000 or
more. If you don't have a shaver,
slice the truffle with a mandoline
set to the thinnest setting, or
with a very sharp knife.

In the fall, the damp forests all over Italy become a hunting ground for precious truffles. This rare luxury cannot be grown on a farm, but must instead be found in the wild around the roots of oak trees, expertly sniffed out by pigs or dogs trained to find them. When the temperature and rainfall are just right, there is an abundance of these woodland delicacies. Whole truffles can fetch outrageous amounts of money (an ounce can cost $100 or more!), especially white ones; black truffles are relatively more affordable but no less delicious. When sliced, they give off intoxicating aromas that are best captured by raining the slivers into melted butter. The flavors are too delicate to be cooked, so simply blooming them in warmed butter lets the truffle express its true essence without losing its spirit. After you toss your pasta with this infused butter, a final flurry of truffle slices creates the ultimate decadence.

Bring a large pot of water to a rolling boil over high heat.

In a large deep sauté pan, melt the butter and a heavy pinch of salt over medium heat. Remove from the heat and shave in around half of the truffle and let it infuse the butter with its aromas while the pasta cooks.

Once the water has reached a rolling boil, season with salt until the water tastes like a seasoned soup. Drop in the pasta and cook until tender, 30 seconds to 1 minute.

Transfer the tagliolini to the sauté pan and toss vigorously in the truffle butter with a few tablespoons of pasta cooking water. The sauce will thicken as the butter and pasta mingle.

Serve with the remaining truffle shaved on top.

RISOTTO *agli* AGRUMI

Serves 4

———

Total prep and cooking time:
1 hour 5 minutes

4 cups Homemade Vegetable Broth
(opposite) or store-bought

3 tablespoons extra-virgin olive oil

1 small white onion, diced

Grated zest of 1 lemon, plus more
for garnish

Grated zest of 1 orange, plus more
for garnish

Sea salt

2 cups rice (Carnaroli or Arborio)

1 cup dry white wine

¼ cup orange juice

3 tablespoons lemon juice

2 tablespoons unsalted butter

60 grams/2 ounces (about ¾ cup)
finely grated Parmigiano-Reggiano

I love experimenting with different ingredients to balance risotto's luscious creaminess, and one of my favorites is fruit. Just as Conchigliette con Pera e Gorgonzola (page 92) is a surprisingly delicious marriage of fruit with pasta, lemon and orange risotto delights the palate with its unique deployment of fruity flavors. Lemons are pretty versatile and no one is really scandalized when they show up in pasta dishes, but oranges? Now that's a first for most Italians. In the end, this risotto is light and super subtly flavored, so if you're skeptical about fruit in your savory dishes, this is a good place to start.

In a medium saucepan, heat the vegetable broth over low heat.

In a large saucepan, heat the olive oil, onion, lemon zest, orange zest, and a heavy pinch of salt over medium-low heat and cook until the onion becomes slightly translucent and releases all of its flavor into the olive oil, 3 to 4 minutes. Increase the heat to medium-high, pour in the rice, and stir to coat in the citrus-infused oil. Continue stirring until the rice is lightly toasted and turns translucent, a couple of minutes. Add the wine and stir until the alcohol aroma dissipates and the liquid reduces by half, about 1½ minutes. Add just enough of the broth to cover the rice. Cook, stirring constantly to release the starches and to keep the rice from sticking to the pan, until the broth has been absorbed, about 2 minutes. Add ½ cup of broth, stirring constantly, and wait until it has been absorbed before adding another ½ cup. Repeat until the rice is very al dente, then stir in the lemon juice and orange juice, cooking until the juice is absorbed and the rice is al dente. You may need to add a bit of extra broth once the juice has been absorbed to finish cooking the rice.

Stir in the butter. Remove from the heat and fold in the Parmigiano-Reggiano.

Serve immediately, garnished with citrus zest.

Homemade
Vegetable Broth

This quick broth gives risotto recipes a unique depth. Make more than you need for this recipe, doubling or tripling the quantities below, so you have some on hand when you are inspired to cook. You can also substitute this broth in recipes that call for meat stock.

Makes 2 quarts

1 medium white onion, halved

2 celery stalks, cut into 2-inch pieces

2 carrots, cut into 2-inch pieces

6 to 8 parsley sprigs

In a medium pot, combine the onion, celery, carrots, and parsley, and 3 quarts of cold water. Bring to a boil over high heat. Reduce the heat to maintain a gentle simmer and cook, uncovered, for 45 minutes. Strain and discard the solids. The broth will keep in a sealed container in the refrigerator for 4 days or in the freezer for 3 months.

PAPPARDELLE *al* RAGÙ *di* CINGHIALE

PAPPARDELLE WITH
WILD BOAR SAUCE

Serves 4

---

*Total prep and cooking time:
14 hours (includes overnight
marinating)*

Alternate pasta shapes:
fresh fettuccine, fresh tagliatelle

1½ pounds wild boar shoulder,
cut into 1-inch pieces

Sea salt

Freshly ground black pepper

3½ cups dry red wine (I like Chianti)

1 tablespoon finely chopped fresh
rosemary

2 small white onions, 1 roughly
chopped and 1 diced

2 bay leaves

4 fresh sage leaves

3 tablespoons extra-virgin olive oil

2 garlic cloves, minced

1 celery stalk, diced

1 carrot, peeled and diced

1 pound fresh pappardelle,
homemade (see page 9)
or store-bought

Fresh oregano leaves, for garnish

Boar meat is incredibly lean. Although they are related to pigs, boars have very little fat, so I have learned some tricks to build flavor in other ways: I choose the right cut, season the meat in advance, and simmer it low and slow for maximum taste and tenderness. I order boar online or place a special order through my butcher and, when available, I choose shoulder, which has a nice fat content. Next, I season the meat overnight so it will be permeated inside and out. Finally, searing the meat, then simmering it in wine and broth, gives it deep flavor and incomparable tenderness. The melt-in-your-mouth sauce clings sensually to the thick strands of pappardelle and will be scooped up by the noodles' flat and wide shape.

Place the boar meat in a medium container and add sea salt, black pepper, 2½ cups of the wine, the rosemary, chopped onion, bay leaves, and sage leaves and refrigerate, covered, overnight (or for at least 12 hours). When ready to cook, remove from the refrigerator and drain (do not rinse the meat).

In a large pot, heat the olive oil and garlic over medium-low heat. Cook until the garlic starts sizzling with little bubbles around it, 1 to 2 minutes. Add the celery, carrot, diced onion, and a heavy pinch of salt. Cook until the vegetables are very soft and just beginning to caramelize, about 15 minutes. Increase the heat to medium-high and add the boar. Season with salt and a scrunch of black pepper and cook until the boar is browned all over. Stir in the remaining 1 cup wine and water to cover, scraping up any browned bits from the bottom of the pot. Once the liquid begins to bubble, reduce the heat to low, cover, and simmer until the meat is tender and nearly falling apart, 2 to 3 hours, adding water as needed to keep the meat mostly submerged.

Once the sauce is nearly done, bring a large pot of water to a rolling boil over high heat. Season with salt until the water tastes like a seasoned soup. Drop in the pasta and cook until tender, 1 to 2 minutes.

Transfer the pasta with a few tablespoons of pasta cooking water to the pot with the ragù and toss to coat.

Serve garnished with oregano leaves.

GORGEOUS TIP

Marinating the boar meat in wine overnight will make it tender and flavorful and tone down any gaminess. Keep the boar in the fridge for at least 12 hours or overnight. No need to rinse the meat before cooking.

Variation

RAGÙ D'ANATRA (DUCK RAGÙ): *If you can't track down boar—or simply have a hunger for duck— you can follow the recipe above and swap out the boar meat for 3 bone- in Moulard or 5 bone-in Peking duck legs to make ragù d'anatra. Follow the boar ragù recipe as written, but cook the duck legs until the meat starts to fall off the bone, about 2 hours, draining off the excess fat. Remove the duck legs from the sauce, pick off and shred the meat (discard the bones), and stir the meat into the sauce.*

LUMACHE *con* LA MENTA

LUMACHE WITH
CHEESY MINT SAUCE

Serves 4

———

Total prep and cooking time:
25 minutes

———

Alternate pasta shapes:
vesuvi, potato gnocchi

Sea salt

1 pound lumache

1 garlic clove, minced

3 tablespoons extra-virgin olive oil

60 grams/2 ounces (about ¾ cup)
finely grated Pecorino Romano

5 ounces provolone, shredded

1 tablespoon roughly chopped
fresh mint leaves, plus whole leaves
for garnish

Freshly ground black pepper

You are about to experience an unexpected twist on mac and cheese. Italy has many recipes that combine pasta with melted cheese sauce, but this recipe is inspired by Rome, where mint grows so boldly you find it all over parks, archeological sites, and even popping up in sidewalk cracks. You will also find *lumache* (snails) in Rome's parks! The pasta shape is reminiscent of these slow-moving gastropods. A flurry of fresh mint turns this simple dish into something elegant, delicate, and unforgettable.

Bring a large pot of water to a rolling boil over high heat. Season with salt until the water tastes like a seasoned soup. Drop in the pasta and cook until al dente.

Meanwhile, in a large deep sauté pan, heat the garlic and olive oil over medium-low heat and cook until the garlic starts sizzling with little bubbles around it, 1 to 2 minutes.

Increase the heat to medium-high and transfer the pasta to the pan along with a ladle (½ cup) of pasta cooking water. Sprinkle on the Pecorino Romano and provolone, stirring with the passion of an Italian and adding more water if needed to melt the cheese and distribute the sauce. Stir in the mint, then baptize with a scrunch of pepper.

Serve garnished with mint leaves.

FETTUCCINE *al* RAGÙ *di* POLPO

FETTUCCINE WITH OCTOPUS SAUCE

Serves 4

Total prep and cooking time:
2 hours 25 minutes

Alternate pasta shapes:
fresh tagliatelle, fresh pappardelle

½ small white onion, diced

½ celery stalk, diced

½ carrot, peeled and diced

Sea salt

¼ cup extra-virgin olive oil

1 octopus, cleaned (see opposite) and cut into ½-inch cubes

Freshly ground black pepper

1 cup dry red wine

1 (15-ounce) can tomato puree

1 tablespoon roughly chopped fresh parsley leaves, plus more for garnish

1 pound fresh fettuccine, homemade (see page 9) or store-bought

This is a story of how an octopus saved what could have been a complicated night. I was with Brook on vacation on the Amalfi coast. After a long day of sightseeing, we arrived at a wonderful hotel on the edge of a cliff. Exhuasted and exhilarated, we walked over to the check-in desk and soon realized that the cost of the hotel was slightly above our means. We tried to run our credit card several times, but there was no magic that could make the sum of money we needed appear.

In between trying to run different cards, the gentleman at the desk asked me what I did, and we got to talking about the passion for cooking that we both shared. I asked him what his favorite recipe was and he said, "Lady, have you heard of an octopus ragù? Mine is the best in the world." He was so passionate about his recipe and so excited to share it with me that he decided to let us stay in his hotel at the rate we could afford. I have made that octopus ragù many times since, so now I can share it with you.

In a large pot, sizzle the onion, celery, carrot, and a heavy pinch of salt in the olive oil over low heat until the vegetables have softened and just begin to caramelize, about 15 minutes. Add the octopus, increase the heat to medium-high, and sizzle for a few minutes. The octopus will begin to release its liquid. Season with salt and a scrunch of pepper. Add the wine and tomato puree and parsley, bring to a boil, and simmer over low heat, uncovered, until the octopus is tender and the flavors have concentrated, about 2 hours. The ragù should have the consistency of a chunky stew. If necessary, turn up the heat to high to evaporate the liquid to reach the desired consistency.

Bring a large pot of water to a rolling boil over high heat. Season with salt until the water tastes like a seasoned soup. Drop in the pasta and cook until tender, 1 to 2 minutes.

Add the pasta and a few tablespoons of pasta cooking water to the octopus sauce and massage together to make your masterpiece.

Serve with parsley leaves sprinkled on top.

HOW TO CLEAN
AN OCTOPUS

I like to clean octopus myself, as I have learned from the fishermen and cooks of Naples, because it makes me feel closer to the Bay and my loved ones nearby. Use a sharp knife to separate the octopus head from the body, just between the eyes and tentacles. Remove the eyes and scrape out the guts and ink sack from the head and discard. Rinse well.

CHAPTER FOUR

FAMILY FIRST

—

*Quick and Easy
Everyday Recipes*

After four years of wedded bliss in a tiny flat in London, Brook and I were on the verge of outgrowing the place in a major way. I was pregnant with my first child, Eleonora, missing home, and desperate to experience the sun, ingredients, and liveliness of Italy again.

So, we packed up and moved to Rome. The transition for me was natural. I was coming home, returning a lot wiser, and with a new appreciation for the city and her classics. Brook had already fallen deeply in love with Italy through our seasonal visits with the family. He dropped everything to make it happen.

We landed in Rome in July, when the markets were absolutely overflowing with eggplants, tomatoes, peppers, zucchini flowers, and figs. I couldn't have dreamed of a better homecoming. My mother let us stay in her apartment near the Vatican, and let me tell you—the kitchen was a major upgrade from the one in our tiny London flat! I loved cooking there, and found even more joy in the kitchen when our daughter was born.

At the same time as my business was thriving, along came my son, Gabriel, and a little after that, my daughter Desiree. It was hard managing a business and the kids. Society is set up to push you toward fast food as stress and time constraints build. Still, cooking remained my passion, and balancing it with both work and motherhood became my mission. I wanted to cook with all the love and energy I could, and I was determined that no corners would be cut. During this time, I stole quick moments to run to the market, and I simplified my recipe collection so meals were as quick and easy as possible while still holding true to their brilliance.

You don't need to have kids for these quick and easy recipes to make sense. The only prerequisite for the dishes in this chapter is a love of pasta, and just a little bit of care to make them just gorgeous.

PESTO *alla* GENOVESE

PASTA WITH BASIL
AND PINE NUT PESTO IN THE
STYLE OF GENOA

Serves 4

———

*Total prep and cooking time:
15 minutes*

———

Alternate pasta shapes:
trofie, trenette

80 grams/3 ounces (about
3 loosely packed cups) fresh basil
leaves, plus more for garnish

50 grams/1¾ ounces (about
5 tablespoons) pine nuts

1 garlic clove

60 grams/2 ounces (about ¾ cup)
finely grated Pecorino Romano

60 grams/2 ounces (about ¾ cup)
finely grated Parmigiano-Reggiano

In Genova, pesto is a religion. The local version is made with a mortar and pestle in stages to make an intensely green raw paste of crushed small-leaf basil, pine nuts, garlic, and cheese emulsified with extra-virgin olive oil. Genovese people are so meticulous about their pesto that they don't allow space for experimentation or shortcuts. But I am here to tell you that you can use a food processor to prepare a pesto that is both fast and delicious—in fact, unless you're a seasoned master, mortar-made pesto probably won't be as smooth, flavorful, or satisfying. In addition to this shortcut, I recommend using a high-quality extra-virgin olive oil, grating the cheeses fresh, plucking the basil leaves directly from a growing plant, and using fresh garlic, never dried! Basically this pesto showcases my pillars of pasta perfection in action. *Pesto alla genovese* is a completely uncooked sauce so it's crucial to use the best ingredients you can find, which will allow the beauty of the flavors to shine through.

Bring a large pot of water to a rolling boil over high heat.

In a food processor or blender, combine the basil, pine nuts, garlic, Pecorino Romano, Parmigiano-Reggiano, and olive oil and blend until the pesto reaches the consistency you desire—I like my pesto to be nearly smooth.

Use a spatula to scrape the pesto into a large bowl. Season with salt to taste.

Once the water has reached a rolling boil, season with salt until the water tastes like a seasoned soup. Drop in the pasta and cook until al dente.

Add a ladle (½ cup) of the tears of the gods to the bowl with the pesto and stir. Add the pasta and toss with the passion of an Italian.

Serve immediately, garnished with basil leaves.

recipe continues

GORGEOUS TIPS

A purist from Genoa may disagree, but I think there's room for some delicious variations in the pesto universe like Pasta Queen Pesto (page 202) and Red Passion Pesto (page 206). In Genoa and the surrounding region of Liguria, playing with a pesto recipe is scandalous. But what's the fun in always following the rules? Once you get to know the proportions of classic pesto, you can play with the ingredients, and even uses. Rather than just using pesto for dressing pasta, why not slather it on a mortadella sandwich or offer it alongside a fresh burrata?

What if I told you that the globally famous pasta dish from Genova is actually only half of the traditional recipe? It's true: The original Genovese preparation also features potatoes and green beans (see photo on page 127). To make the real classic, peel and cut 4 small Yukon Gold potatoes into bite-sized pieces and snap the ends off ½ pound green beans. Boil the potatoes in a large pot of salted water for 15 minutes before you add the pasta and green beans. Drain and toss the potatoes, pasta, and green beans with the pesto and serve.

TIMBALLO *di* PASTA

LEFTOVER PASTA BAKE

Serves 2

Total prep and cooking time:
20 minutes

2 teaspoons extra-virgin olive oil,
plus more for greasing

2 cups leftover pasta

2 ounces salami, ham, or sausage,
cut into ½-inch pieces

2 ounces cheese of your choice,
cut into ½-inch pieces (I like
Fontina)

2 ounces thinly sliced provolone or
torn mozzarella

Fresh basil leaves, for garnish

I never let pasta go to waste, especially when I'm pressed for time but still want to put something delicious on the table for family. Whenever I have leftover pasta, I look in the refrigerator and take out all the little bits of other left-over food I can find: an end of a salami, half a ball of mozzarella cheese, a tiny piece of Parmigiano-Reggiano, hard-boiled egg, a bit of provolone—whatever I think I can use up and that will go together. I mix all my found ingredients with the pasta, lace it with a drizzle of olive oil, and blanket it in a layer of my favorite cheeses. I bake it to perfection, crown it with basil, and whisper, "Just gorgeous."

The beauty of this timballo is that it's a lesson in not wasting food and it gives new life to leftovers. However, it's just a blueprint—so get creative with whatever ingredients you have in the fridge. If you have veggies, cheese, cold cuts, leftover meatballs, whatever, you can transform them into something new by baking them with pasta. There are no rules at all; just let your appetite decide and follow your heart. My only advice is to always use a melting cheese such as Fontina or scamorza to bind it all together. This recipe is based on two portions of leftover pasta, but you can always double or triple the amounts of the other ingredients based on how much pasta you have.

Preheat the oven to 400°F.

Oil a baking dish that's large enough to accommodate your pasta and other fillings so they are no more than 1½ inches high.

In a bowl large enough to accommodate them, combine the pasta, salami, cheese of choice, and any other leftover items you might be using. Pour them into the oiled baking dish, drizzle with the olive oil, and cover with the sliced provolone.

Bake until the pasta is warmed through and the cheese on top has melted, about 15 minutes.

Serve garnished with fresh basil leaves.

TORTELLINI *alla* PANNA

TORTELLINI
IN A CREAM SAUCE
WITH CHEESE

Serves 4

Total prep and cooking time:
20 minutes

Alternate pasta shapes:
fresh tagliolini, fresh fettuccine

5 cups meat broth from tortellini
filling preparation or 5 cups water

1 cup heavy cream

300 grams/10½ ounces
(about 3¾ cups) finely grated
Parmigiano-Reggiano

1 pound fresh meat-filled
tortellini, homemade (page 21)
or store-bought

Most of my cooking knowledge comes from the great women in my family and through my own trial and error. However, I have an obsession with professional cooks, and I admire a handful whom I have studied painstakingly. One of these is Chef Massimo Bottura. I feel we share the same humble origins and passion for food culture. This recipe is included in homage to him.

To make *tortellini alla panna*, you can go two routes: Either make fresh tortellini from scratch for a real labor of love, or purchase store-bought tortellini for a quicker option. Whichever route you choose, the fast and flirty sauce clings to the gorgeous curves and folds of the pasta in the most tantalizing way.

In a large pot, bring the meat broth to a rolling boil over high heat.

Meanwhile, heat the heavy cream in a medium pot over medium-high heat and simmer, stirring frequently until it thickens, about 5 minutes. Stir in the Parmigiano-Reggiano. Turn off the heat and carefully use a hand mixer to mix until smooth and airy. Keep warm over a low heat.

Once the broth has reached a rolling boil, drop in the tortellini. Allow the water to return to a boil, reduce the heat to low, and cook until the tortellini float and are tender, 1½ to 2 minutes.

Add the tortellini and a tablespoon of pasta cooking water to the cream sauce. Swirl gently to coat as the sauce thickens.

Serve.

LINGUINE *al* TONNO

LINGUINE WITH
CANNED TUNA

Serves 4

Total prep and cooking time:
25 minutes

Alternate pasta shapes:
spaghetti, penne

2 (5-ounce) cans tuna
(I like yellowfin), preferably
packed in high-quality extra-virgin
olive oil, drained

1 tablespoon lemon juice

1 tablespoon roughly
chopped fresh parsley leaves,
plus more for garnish

1 small white onion, diced

Sea salt

3 tablespoons extra-virgin olive oil

½ cup olives (I like Gaeta and
Kalamata), rinsed and pitted

2 tablespoons capers
(rinsed and soaked if salt-packed,
drained if in brine)

1 cup dry white wine

1 pound linguine

It is quite a sight to arrive in Puglia and be blinded by its predominantly white architectural beauty. I was just a kid when I met Michelina, my stepmother Angela's mom, who quickly became another nonna to me. She took me on as if she had known me forever. When I visited her in Puglia, we stayed in a *trullo* (a small domed house with a sharp triangular roof) by the sea. My brother and I would spend our days diving from rocks into the deep blue ocean, and we would come back to the trullo for lunch, where Michelina and Angela had prepared the most amazing *linguine al tonno*—a quick dish that is a flavorful blend of canned yellowfin tuna, onions, capers, and olives. Michelina would always spike the sauce with a glass of white wine, which gave the tuna sauce a gorgeously subtle fruitiness from the grapes.

Bring a large pot of water to a rolling boil over high heat.

Meanwhile, in a medium bowl, combine the tuna, lemon juice, and parsley in a medium bowl.

In a large deep sauté pan, cook the onion and a heavy pinch of salt in the olive oil over medium-low heat until the onion becomes slightly translucent and releases all of its flavor into the olive oil, 3 to 4 minutes.

Add the tuna mixture, olives, and capers to the sauté pan. Increase the heat to medium-high, add the wine, and cook until the alcohol aroma has dissipated and the liquid has reduced by half, about 1½ minutes. Reduce the heat to low and simmer for 10 minutes, adding pasta cooking water to the pan a ladle (½ cup) at a time if it gets dry.

Once the water has reached a rolling boil, season with salt until the water tastes like a seasoned soup. Drop in the pasta and cook until al dente.

Add the pasta to the pan and toss to coat.

Serve garnished with parsley.

GORGEOUS TIP

Let's face it. Canned tuna doesn't conjure nostalgic vacation memories for everyone, and a lot of canned tuna out there doesn't taste very good. I recommend buying high-quality tuna—Gustiamo.com is great for Italian brands, while Formaggio Kitchen stocks Spanish *conservas* (tinned fish) as well as Italian. Because tuna is such a central ingredient in this dish, use the best you can find. If you can only find supermarket canned albacore, which tastes quite fishy, cut the fishiness with an extra squeeze of lemon.

PASTA CAPRESE

PENNONI WITH
MOZZARELLA, TOMATO,
AND BASIL

Serves 4

———

Total prep and cooking time:
20 minutes

———

Alternate pasta shapes:
penne, farfalle

Sea salt

1 pound pennoni

¼ cup extra-virgin olive oil, plus
more for drizzling

1 pound grape tomatoes, halved

8 to 10 fresh basil leaves, torn, plus
more for garnish

14 ounces fresh mozzarella,
torn into 1-inch pieces, at room
temperature

Sea salt

GORGEOUS TIP

Make sure the cheese you use is at
room temperature when you add
it to the hot pasta. It won't fully
melt, but it will soften pleasingly
when it meets the hot pasta.

The soft mozzarella, tangy tomatoes, and fragrant basil of
this pasta salad will awaken your inner Italian and transport
you directly to Capri, the island off the coast of Campania that
gives Caprese salad and this dish their names. One legend has
it that the combination of mozzarella, tomatoes, and basil was
invented at the Quisisana Hotel in Capri for the benefit of a
famous philosopher and anti-pasta activist Filippo Tommaso
Marinetti. He would have hated this book—or even fallen back
in love with pasta after reading this recipe. Another myth
states a bricklayer wanted a patriotic sandwich filling that
evoked the green, white, and red of the Italian flag.

Like we do in Italy, only use tomatoes at their peak
of freshness, when they are bursting with sweetness and
acidity—out-of-season tomatoes will taste flavorless and sad
by comparison. Let the drained *pennoni* (large penne) gently
warm this lightning-fast no-cook sauce. Serve it at a picnic or
barbecue, or pack it in a plastic container like an Italian nonna
and take it with you to the beach. Then eat with reckless
abandon while lounging by the sea, as the salt water dries on
your sun-kissed body.

Bring a large pot of water to a rolling boil over high heat.
Season with salt until the water tastes like a seasoned soup.
Drop in the pasta and cook until al dente.

Meanwhile, in a large bowl, combine the olive oil, tomatoes,
basil, and mozzarella. Kiss with a flurry of sea salt, then toss
in the drained pasta, which will awaken the basil aromas with
its warmth as it gently softens the mozzarella. If you don't mix
the ingredients with the drained pasta right away, drizzle some
olive oil over the pasta so it doesn't stick together.

Serve garnished with basil leaves and a drizzle of olive oil.

LASAGNA VEGETARIANA
con SFOGLIA VERDE

❁

VEGETARIAN LASAGNA
WITH SPINACH PASTA

*Makes one 9 × 13-inch lasagna
(8 servings)*

———

*Total prep and cooking time:
1 hour 15 minutes*

———

Alternate pasta shape:
sfoglia all'uovo

4 medium zucchini, thinly sliced

Sea salt

1 tablespoon extra-virgin olive oil

1 pound fresh spinach or 1 cup
frozen spinach, thawed and finely
chopped

250 grams/9 ounces (about 3 cups)
fresh ricotta

2½ cups Béchamel (page 72)

250 grams/9 ounces (about 3 cups)
finely grated Parmigiano-Reggiano

Sfoglia Verde (page 16), rolled
out and cut into strips you can
assemble to measure the size of
your baking dish, or store-bought
fresh pasta sheets

Everyone loves lasagna and its layers upon layers of lusciousness. There are a lot of different spins on the classic lasagna of Bologna made with meat ragù and béchamel, such as Lasagna al Ragù di Lady Caterina (page 71). This vegetarian version is a perfect example of a traditional recipe with a sensational twist. My filling is ricotta and spinach with béchamel, making it a quicker and lighter lasagna that's ideal for weeknights, especially if you substitute store-bought pasta sheets for homemade fresh spinach-tinted pasta. Whether you build every element from scratch or cut a few corners, this vegetarian dish is a crowd-pleaser and a cheeky way to get the kiddies to eat their veggies.

Preheat the oven to 375°F.

Spread out the zucchini on a flat surface and lightly salt both sides. Let sit for 30 minutes, then pat dry. Brush the olive oil over a grill pan over medium heat. Grill the zucchini slices on both sides, 3 to 4 minutes per side. Set aside.

If you are using fresh spinach, bring a large pot of water to a rolling boil over high heat. (If you are using frozen spinach, skip this step.) When the water has reached a rolling boil, season with salt until the water tastes like a seasoned soup. Boil the spinach until the stems become tender, about 2 minutes, then cool and squeeze out any liquid with a cheesecloth or kitchen towel.

In a medium bowl, combine the spinach, ricotta, and a heavy pinch of salt.

Spoon ½ cup of béchamel over the bottom of a 9 × 13-inch baking dish. Make a layer in this order: A layer of pasta (no need to cook fresh pasta in advance, as it cooks in the moisture of the filling); you may need to use several pieces to cover the area of the baking dish. Follow with one-third

of the ricotta/spinach mixture, one-quarter of the zucchini,
½ cup béchamel, and one-quarter of the Parmigiano-Reggiano.
Repeat this layering two more times (for a total of 3 layers). Top
with a final piece of pasta and the remaining zucchini, ½ cup
béchamel, and remaining Parmigiano-Reggiano.

Cover the baking dish with foil and bake for 30 minutes. Uncover
the baking dish, then continue baking until the edges of the pasta
are curled up and browned, 30 to 40 minutes longer.

Allow the lasagna to rest for about 20 minutes before serving in
slices.

PASTINA *in* BRODO

Serves 4

———

*Total prep and cooking time:
2 hours 20 minutes*

———

Alternate pasta shapes:
tubettini, margheritine, orzo,
maltagliati

4 quarts Homemade Chicken Stock
(opposite) or store-bought

Sea salt

1 pound stelline

Roughly chopped vegetables and
shredded meat (optional; from
homemade chicken stock)

Finely grated Parmigiano-Reggiano,
for dusting

Extra-virgin olive oil, for drizzling

My Auntie Pina is a middle school teacher, and she has always been an amazing multitasker. She has three children—my cousins whom I grew up with—and even though she always worked full-time, she never missed cooking a family dinner. I lived with her every summer when I was a young teenager, and I can still smell her *pastina in brodo* just thinking about it. The ultimate act of love from my auntie was to bring Parmigiano-Reggiano and formaggino to the table and place it right in the center of the broth for us to savor.

The way I prepare pastina in brodo depends on whom I am serving it to. When I make it for my kids, I strain the broth to eliminate the cooked vegetables. Otherwise it's much harder to get them to eat this. Sometimes I add shredded chicken. If I am serving it to Brook or a friend, I will remove the cooked vegetables, chop them into tiny pieces, and return them to the pot. I will often add a 1-inch piece of fresh turmeric or 1 teaspoon of powdered turmeric about 15 minutes before the broth is ready, to add its wonderful flavor.

In a medium pot, bring the stock to a rolling boil over medium-high heat. Season with salt to taste and add the stelline. If you made homemade stock, add the chopped vegetables and shredded meat (if using). Cook until the stelline are al dente.

Serve blanketed with a dusting of Parmigiano-Reggiano and a drizzle of extra-virgin olive oil.

GORGEOUS TIPS

Occasionally, I will add peeled potatoes cut into ½-inch cubes to the broth 25 minutes before the pasta goes in so they are soft and tender by the time the stelline are cooked. I love to add a dollop of Formaggini Crema Bel Paese to the bowl, a subtly sweet, semi-soft cheese from Italy that's also available in the States, because it adds a gorgeous contrast to the chicken broth.

If you are using store-bought stock and wish to have vegetables in your broth, cut a peeled carrot and a celery stalk into ½-inch pieces and cook in the broth until very soft, then add the pasta.

Homemade Chicken Stock

When I make homemade chicken stock for a soup like Pastina in Brodo (opposite), I shred the cooked chicken with a fork and chop the vegetables and add them the dish. Otherwise I save the chicken for chicken salad. If you prefer, you can use raw chicken bones or whole chicken breasts instead of a whole chicken.

Makes about 4 quarts

---

1 whole chicken

2 carrots, halved

2 celery stalks, halved

2 medium white onions, quartered

8 to 10 sprigs fresh parsley

2 (2.4-ounce) rinds of Parmigiano-Reggiano (optional)

Place the chicken, carrots, celery, onions, parsley, and Parmigiano-Reggiano rind (if using), in a large pot and add about 4½ quarts water to cover. Slowly bring the water to a gentle simmer over low heat, skimming off any scum that rises to the top using a spoon. Cook at a low simmer, uncovered, for about 2 hours.

Strain the stock. If using for a soup, save the vegetables and chicken to chop or shred and add to the soup.

RIGATONI *alla* BOSCAIOLA

RIGATONI WITH PANCETTA,
PEAS, MUSHROOMS,
AND CREAM

Serves 4

Total prep and cooking time:
35 minutes

Alternate pasta shapes:
mezze maniche, tortellini, fettuccine

2 tablespoons unsalted butter

4 ounces pancetta, cut into
½-inch cubes

2 garlic cloves, minced

2 teaspoons roughly chopped fresh
parsley leaves

1 pound mushrooms
(I like cremini and porcini), cut into
bite-sized pieces

1½ cups fresh or frozen peas
(if using fresh, cook in salted water
until tender, about 2 minutes)

Sea salt

1 cup dry white wine

2 cups heavy cream

1 pound rigatoni

Finely grated Parmigiano-Reggiano,
for dusting

Many Italian dishes are named for an occupation, like Spaghettoni alla Puttanesca (page 68). In this case, it's rigatoni in the style of the woodsman. Imagine what a burly, outdoorsy Italian man would eat to warm his bones while out harvesting timber in the forest, or how he might nourish himself before a hunt, and you've got this dish: pasta drenched in a cream sauce of pancetta, peas, and mushrooms. The cream gives it warmth, the peas add texture and sweetness, the pancetta delivers a savory note, and the mushrooms—of course—represent the woodsman's beloved forest. This combination of ingredients offers the perfect burst of energy needed for any difficult task. The dish is earthy, sweet, and powerful, just like you are!

Bring a large pot of water to a rolling boil over high heat.

In a large deep sauté pan, heat the butter and pancetta over low heat and cook until the pancetta starts releasing its fat and begins to take color, about 5 minutes. Add the garlic over medium-low heat and cook until it starts sizzling with little bubbles around it, 1 to 2 minutes. Increase the heat to medium-high and add the parsley to infuse the pan with its sweet herbal flavor. Add the mushrooms and peas and season with salt. Add the wine and simmer until the alcohol aroma dissipates and the liquid reduces by half, about 1½ minutes. Add the cream and a heavy pinch of salt. Simmer, stirring frequently, until the sauce thickens enough to coat the back of a spoon, about 5 minutes.

Once the water has reached a rolling boil, season with salt until the water tastes like a seasoned soup. Drop in the pasta and cook until al dente.

Add the pasta to the sauté pan and massage together until the pasta is drenched in this hunter's sauce, adding pasta cooking water a tablespoon at a time if needed to bind the sauce to the pasta.

Serve immediately with Parmigiano-Reggiano dusted on top.

FRITTATA *di* PASTA

Serves 4

———

Total prep and cooking time:
35 minutes

———

Alternate pasta shapes:
ziti, pennoni

Sea salt

1 pound spaghetti

1 tablespoon unsalted butter

5 large eggs

Freshly ground black pepper

100 grams/3½ ounces
(about 1¼ cups) finely grated
Parmigiano-Reggiano

¼ cup cubed (¼-inch) salami

6 ounces fresh mozzarella, cut into
¼-inch cubes

Extra-virgin olive oil, for greasing

Fresh basil leaves, for garnish

Centuries ago, pasta was sold by street vendors and eaten as fast food by the Neapolitan working class who could barely afford good ingredients, much less utensils. They would use their hands to feed themselves long strands of spaghetti, which they would hold above their heads and lower into their open mouths in lieu of using a fork. Posters and paintings decorating the walls of Italian trattorias show this uniquely Neapolitan custom. Always creative and curious, Neapolitans eventually invented a way to make a portion of spaghetti truly portable: by cooking it with eggs into a sort of omelet, which could be cut into slices for enjoying on the go. There's nothing more satisfying than whipping up a frittata before hitting the beach and devouring it by the slice while you are sunbathing.

Bring a large pot of water to a rolling boil over high heat. Season with salt until the water tastes like a seasoned soup. Drop in the pasta and cook until al dente. Drain the pasta and return to the pot with the butter, stirring to coat.

In a medium bowl, combine the eggs, a scrunch of pepper, the Parmigiano-Reggiano, salami, mozzarella, and a heavy pinch of salt.

Grease the bottom and sides of a 12-inch nonstick skillet with olive oil. Transfer the pasta in an even layer to the pan. Pour the egg mixture over the pasta. Set the pan over low heat and cook until the edges are set and the center is mostly cooked, about 10 minutes. Remove from the heat.

Gently slide the frittata out of the pan and onto a plate using a spatula. The uncooked top of the frittata will be facing up. Carefully invert the skillet over the plate and in one quick and confident movement, flip over the pan and the plate together. The frittata should land in the pan with the cooked side facing up.

recipe continues

GORGEOUS TIPS

Return the pan to low heat and cook until the bottom of the frittata begins to turn golden, about 6 minutes. Use a heatproof spatula to lift the edge of the frittata to check for doneness. Remove from the heat and allow the frittata to rest for a few minutes before slicing.

Serve warm or at room temperature cut into wedges garnished with fresh basil leaves.

You can either use leftover spaghetti with this recipe, giving it a new life and a new texture, or you can make it with pasta cooked from scratch, as I do.

The frittata flip in this recipe requires a bit of practice and a lot of confidence. If you don't want to give it a shot, you can finish cooking the frittata in the oven. When you put the water for the pasta on to boil, preheat the oven to 375°F. Then cook the frittata on the stovetop in an ovenproof pan. Once the eggs begin to set around the edges, remove from the heat and transfer to the oven. Bake the frittata until the edges start to come away from the sides of the pan and the frittata is totally set in the middle, 10 to 15 minutes.

Remove the pan from the oven and allow the frittata to cool before serving. To unmold, run a spatula around the edges and underneath the frittata and slide it onto a serving plate.

TORTELLINI *in* BRODO

TORTELLINI IN BROTH

Serves 4

———

Total prep and cooking time:
4 hours 5 minutes

1 pound bone-in capon parts

1 pound bone-in beef (I like ribs)

1 carrot, halved

2 celery stalks, halved

1 small white onion, halved

5 or 6 springs fresh parsley

1 bay leaf

1 teaspoon black peppercorns

1 (1.2-ounce) rind of Parmigiano-
Reggiano (optional)

Sea salt

1 pound fresh tortellini,
homemade (page 21) or
store-bought

GORGEOUS TIP

I always buy big hunks of
Parmigiano-Reggiano, which
include a tough rind. Once I have
used the softer gratable part, I set
aside the rind to use in broths to
deepen and intensify their flavor.
I don't use the actual cheese.

At Christmas, families all over Italy prepare laborious feasts.
It's one of my favorite times of year, when the family dedicates
days on end to making dozens of holiday specialties. One
lovingly prepared dish is *tortellini in brodo*: very tiny, meat-
filled dumplings that bob in a savory broth. Pasta fillings for
this classic change from city to city—and even from home to
home—but meat and cheese are common to them all.

You don't have to wait until Christmas to prepare tortellini
in brodo. And you don't have to make the tortellini and capon
stock from scratch unless you want to. Store-bought meat-
filled tortellini and homemade or store-bought vegetable broth
or chicken stock are perfectly fine substitutes. But when I am
making the traditional version at Christmas, only homemade
will do. The tradition calls for *brodo di cappone*, stock made
from the meat and bones of a capon (castrated rooster), which
delivers rich and unparalleled flavor. You may have to special-
order that from your butcher, so be sure to do so well in advance.
And it never hurts to make more than you need for one recipe
so you can freeze the extra and use it for another time.

Place the capon, beef, carrot, celery, onion, parsley, bay leaf,
peppercorns, and Parmigiano-Reggiano rind (if using) in a
large pot with about 6 quarts water to cover. Slowly bring the
water to a gentle simmer over low heat, skimming off any scum
that rises to the top. Cook at a low simmer, uncovered, until the
meats are very tender, 3 to 4 hours.

Strain the stock, discard the vegetables, and transfer it to a
clean pot. (Save the capon meat and beef for another use,
picking the meat off the bone.)

Bring the stock to a rolling boil over medium heat and season
with salt to taste. Add the tortellini and cook until they float
and are tender, 2 to 3 minutes.

Serve the dish immediately to prevent the pasta from
overcooking in the hot broth.

SPAGHETTI *allo* SCOGLIO

SPAGHETTI WITH CLAMS,
MUSSELS, SHRIMP,
LANGOUSTINES, AND
CALAMARI

Serves 4

Total prep and cooking time:
30 minutes

Alternate pasta shapes:
paccheri, linguine, calamarata

½ cup extra-virgin olive oil

2 garlic cloves, minced

2 cups cherry tomatoes, halved

2 teaspoons finely chopped
fresh parsley leaves, plus more for
garnish

Sea salt

1 pound clams, rinsed (see How to
Clean Clams, page 55)

1 pound mussels, beards removed
and scrubbed

1 cup dry white wine

¾ pound medium shrimp, peeled
and deveined

1 pound head and shell-on
langoustines, rinsed

½ pound calamari, cut into rings

1 pound spaghetti

Sometimes gestures of affection are subtle. That is not the case with *spaghetti allo scoglio*, a seafood pasta that is a luxurious symphony of seafood. I remember visiting the markets in London where my husband and I first lived together, and although the produce was a bit grim by my Italian standards, the seafood was absolutely gorgeous. I would visit the local fishmonger and as I patiently waited in the queue, I would calculate in my head exactly how many shrimp, langoustines, clams, mussels, and calamari I could afford with the quid in my purse. Some days it was more and some days it was less. But even in the less flush moments, the love and attention that I would give to each ingredient was code for how deeply I cared for Brook and anyone else I was feeding. Whether you intend to impress a lover or a friend—or simply wish to practice an act of self-love—harnessing the flavors of the sea with this dish is guaranteed to satisfy. The key to this recipe is to finish cooking the pasta in the clam and mussel juices to infuse it with the essence of the sea. As a bonus, it's fast to pull together, though you would never know it from its deeply developed flavors.

Bring a large pot of water to a rolling boil over high heat.

In a large deep sauté pan, heat the olive oil and garlic over medium-low heat and cook until the garlic starts sizzling with little bubbles around it, 1 to 2 minutes. Increase the heat to medium-high, add the tomatoes and parsley, season with salt, and cook until the tomatoes just begin to soften, about 2 minutes. Add the clams, mussels, and wine. Cook, uncovered, using tongs to transfer the mussels and clams to a medium bowl as soon as they open. Some will open within 30 seconds, others after about 3 minutes. Discard any mussels or clams that do not open. Pick three-quarters of the mussel and clam meats from their shells, discarding the shells, and set aside. Leave the remaining mussels and clams as is.

recipe continues

Add the shrimp, langoustines, and calamari to the sauté pan and cook until the shrimp are just cooked through and turn pink, 3 to 4 minutes.

Once the water has reached a rolling boil, season with salt until the water tastes like a seasoned soup. Drop in the pasta and cook until very al dente (a little more than half the recommended cooking time).

Transfer the pasta to the sauté pan and cook until al dente, stirring frequently as it absorbs the liquid and adding more pasta cooking water as needed to loosen the sauce and cook the pasta.

Just before serving the pasta, add all of the cooked mussels and clams back to the pan and toss well to warm them.

Serve sprinkled with a flurry of parsley.

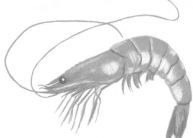

HOW TO DEVEIN SHRIMP

Use a knife to cut a shallow incision along the dark line that runs along the back of the shrimp. This is the shrimp's intestine. Use the tip of the knife to gently extract the dark vein.

FETTUCCINE ALFREDO

**FETTUCCINE
WITH BUTTER AND
PARMIGIANO-REGGIANO**

Serves 4

---

*Total prep and cooking time:
15 minutes*

Alternate pasta shape:
tagliatelle

2 sticks (8 ounces) unsalted butter

Sea salt

1 pound fresh fettuccine,
homemade (see page 9) or
store-bought

250 grams/9 ounces (about 3 cups)
finely grated Parmigiano-Reggiano

When I moved to America, I was shocked that fettuccine Alfredo was on menus everywhere. Barely anyone in Rome knows this dish, even though it was invented there one hundred years ago. The reason it's off most Romans' radar is because it is the specialty of just two competing restaurants in the center of town—Alfredo alla Scrofa and Il Vero Alfredo. Like all famous dishes, fettuccine Alfredo has an origin story. A century ago, a man named Alfredo di Lelio wanted to give his wife the strength to recover from an illness, so he cooked her the richest dish he could imagine: pasta tossed with melted butter and grated Parmigiano-Reggiano. It was so effective and delicious that he put it on the menu of his own trattoria, Alfredo alla Scrofa, and named it for himself. He sold his restaurant, which continued to serve his specialty, and later opened a competing trattoria—Il Vero Alfredo—nearby. To this day, the two Alfredo restaurants serve their signature dishes tossed tableside until the fettuccine are drenched in a thick emulsion of butter and cheese, which is so rich that you don't need even a drop of cream. Di Lelio's granddaughters, whom I had the pleasure of meeting, now run the institution, dutifully carrying on the family tradition, and they showed me their pasta-tossing tricks so I can pull together this 5-minute pasta dish for my own family just as they do in Rome.

Bring a large pot of water to a rolling boil over high heat.

Meanwhile, in a large deep sauté pan, melt the butter.

Once the water has reached a rolling boil, season with salt until the water tastes like a seasoned soup. Drop in the fettuccine and cook until they are tender, about 2 minutes.

Transfer the pasta to the pan with the melted butter and toss gently to coat. Remove from the heat and stir in the Parmigiano-Reggiano, tossing gently until the sauce is thick and creamy. Add pasta water a tablespoon at a time as necessary to make the sauce unbelievably silky. Serve.

WATCH THIS RECIPE

CONCHIGLIONI *al* FORNO
con POMODORO E RICOTTA

BAKED STUFFED SHELLS
WITH TOMATO AND RICOTTA

Serves 4

Total prep and cooking time:
1 hour 10 minutes

2 tablespoons extra-virgin olive oil

½ small white onion, diced

Sea salt

3 fresh basil leaves, plus more for
garnish

1 (15-ounce) can tomato puree

1 pound conchiglioni

1 pound fresh ricotta

1 pound mozzarella, cut into
½-inch pieces

Freshly ground black pepper

60 grams/2 ounces (about ¾ cup)
finely grated Parmigiano-Reggiano

Conchiglioni (big shells) belong to a family of pasta shapes from around Naples that recall the sea. When you live near the curving Bay of Naples or the lapping waters of the Sorrentine Peninsula or the Amalfi Coast, it's natural that pasta forms reflect the territory they come from. These large, shell-shaped pastas are cooked on the stove until very al dente, then finished in the oven to absorb the gorgeous flavors and moisture from their mozzarella and ricotta filling and the fresh tomatoes of the sultry sauce. The additional mozzarella sprinkled on top melts to create a luscious cheese pull that will transform any weekday meal into an event and have your guests begging for more.

Preheat the oven to 400°F.

Bring a large pot of water to a rolling boil over high heat.

Meanwhile, in a medium saucepan or pot, heat the olive oil, onion, and a pinch of salt over medium-low heat until the onion becomes slightly translucent and releases all of its flavor into the olive oil, 3 to 4 minutes. Add the basil and sizzle in the oil until fragrant, about 15 seconds. Increase the heat to medium-high, add the tomato puree and a heavy pinch of salt, and cook just until the puree loses its raw flavor, about 10 minutes. Taste the sauce and stir in more salt if you feel it needs more seasoning.

Once the water has reached a rolling boil, season with salt until the water tastes like a seasoned soup. Drop in the pasta and cook until very al dente (a little more than half the recommended cooking time). Drain and set aside.

While the pasta cooks, in a medium bowl, combine the ricotta and two-thirds of the mozzarella and season with salt and a scrunch of pepper.

Spoon a thin layer of tomato sauce on the bottom of a baking pan large enough to fit the pasta snugly in a single layer. Spoon the ricotta and mozzarella mixture into the pasta shells, filling them completely, and arrange in the pan. Drizzle with the remaining tomato sauce and sprinkle with the remaining mozzarella and the Parmigiano-Reggiano.

Cover with foil and bake for 20 minutes. Uncover and continue baking until the mozzarella starts to form a golden crust, about 5 minutes longer.

Let the shells rest in the pan for 10 minutes, then serve garnished with fresh basil leaves. Eat voraciously with your hands.

INSALATA *di* PASTA E TONNO

ITALIAN TUNA PASTA SALAD

Serves 4

———

Total prep and cooking time:
25 minutes

———

Alternate pasta shape:
fusilli

———

Sea salt

1 pound farfalle

¼ cup plus 2 tablespoons extra
virgin olive oil

2 sprigs fresh oregano, picked

4 to 6 fresh basil leaves, torn, plus
whole leaves for garnish

2 (5-ounce) cans tuna (I prefer tuna
in oil), drained and flaked

½ cup olives (I like Gaeta or
Kalamata)

½ pound cherry tomatoes, halved

8 ounces fresh mozzarella, cut into
¼-inch cubes, at room temperature

Freshly ground black pepper

Every summer in Rome, cafés stock their display cases with specialties that are suited to the steamy temperatures. One of these seasonal classics is pasta salad mixed with tuna and other ingredients that change from place to place. This recipe is my favorite version, a mixture of savory oil-packed tuna, briny olives, sweet tomatoes, and springy mozzarella. All Italian summer pasta salads are served at room temperature, and they are just perfect for a quick and light lunch or a picnic.

Feel free to use this recipe as a blueprint for your own pasta salad and then get creative with the ingredients. Some great additions are cubes of Emmentaler cheese, capers, arugula, pearl onions, pickles, or even canned corn. There's lots of room for creativity here with bright and colorful ingredients that are a feast for the eyes.

Bring a large pot of water to a rolling boil over high heat. Season with salt until it tastes like a seasoned soup. Drop in the pasta and cook until al dente. Drain and transfer to a large bowl.

Drizzle ¼ cup of the olive oil over the pasta and stir in the oregano and basil, infusing the oil and the pasta with their gorgeous herbaceous aromas. Stir in the tuna, olives, tomatoes, and mozzarella, tossing with the passion of an Italian. Drizzle over the remaining 2 tablespoons olive oil, then season with salt and a scrunch of pepper.

Serve at room temperature garnished with fresh basil leaves.

PASTINA RISOTTATA

PASTA COOKED LIKE
RISOTTO

Serves 4

———

*Total prep and cooking time:
25 minutes*

Sea salt

1 shallot, diced

3 tablespoons extra-virgin olive oil

6 to 8 fresh basil leaves, torn, plus
whole leaves for garnish

3½ cups Fresh Tomato Sauce
(opposite) or 1 (24-ounce) jar
unseasoned sauce

1 pound orzo

60 grams/2 ounces (about ¾ cup)
finely grated Pecorino Romano, plus
more for dusting

GORGEOUS TIP

I chose orzo for this dish because
it looks a bit like the rice used for
risotto. *Orzo* in Italian actually
means "barley," and the pasta is
so named because it is shaped like
unhulled barley grains—which
are harvested from shimmering
rows across Southern Italy.

Risottare is the Italian verb for a cooking method borrowed
from risotto. In other words, to make a dish *risottato* (the related
adjective!), the main ingredient—in this case, pasta—must be
slowly simmered while adding small amounts of hot liquid at
a time until it is absorbed and everything is cooked through.
This technique allows the pasta to release its silky starches and
take on the flavor of any other ingredients as it cooks, giving
the finished dish an incredibly creamy texture without the
addition of butter or cream. It's a very unusual way of cooking
pasta, but it's also one that I absolutely love, especially because
it's such an easy one-pot meal. You'll find the *risottato* method
also used to make The Lazy Princess (page 210), Pasta con le
Patate (page 77), and Creamy Broccoli Delight (page 232), all
of which cook the pasta directly in their sauce.

In a medium pot, bring 4 cups of the blanching water from
the Fresh Tomato Sauce (or plain water if using store-bought
sauce) to a rolling boil over high heat.

In a large sauce pan, sizzle the shallot and a pinch of salt in
the olive oil over low heat until bubbles form, 1 to 2 minutes.
Increase the heat to medium and add the basil leaves, sizzling
until fragrant, about 15 seconds. Add the tomato sauce and a
bit more salt. Increase the heat to medium and simmer gently,
adding the orzo after a minute or two. Cook the orzo, adding
boiling water as needed to cover the pasta, and to keep the
sauce juicy and luscious, until the pasta is al dente. Remove
from the heat and stir in the Pecorino Romano.

Serve garnished with basil leaves and dusted with Pecorino
Romano.

Fresh Tomato Sauce

Makes about 4 cups

———

3½ pounds ripe Roma tomatoes
Sea salt

Cut an "X" into the butt end of each tomato. Bring a large pot of water to a rolling boil, then add the tomatoes and cook for 1 minute. Drain, reserving the tomato cooking water for the pastina risottata, and shock the tomatoes in an ice bath. Remove the skins and discard them. To remove the seeds from the tomatoes, halve the tomatoes lengthwise and use a spoon to scoop out the seeds. Season with salt to taste. Blend in a food processor until smooth.

The uncooked tomato sauce will keep in a sealed container in the refrigerator for 4 to 5 days.

CANDELE E CARNE *alla* PIZZAIOLA

PIZZA-STYLE PASTA
AND MEAT

Serves 4

———

Total prep and cooking time:
25 minutes

———

Alternate pasta shapes:
ziti, rigatoni, penne

2 garlic cloves, minced

¼ cup extra-virgin olive oil

1 (28-ounce) can tomato puree

Sea salt and freshly ground
black pepper

1 teaspoon fresh oregano, plus a
sprig for garnish

1 pound round steak, thinly sliced

1 pound candele lunghe, broken
into 3-inch pieces

GORGEOUS TIP

The type of pasta that I use
for this dish is called *candele*,
or "candles." The long tubes
resembling candles are broken
by hand into smaller pieces,
making jagged edges that act as
funnels to scoop up the savory
meat sauce.

In the south of Italy, there is a dish called *carne alla pizzaiola* (pizza-style meat) because it is cooked in a sauce that evokes a pizza topping: tomatoes, garlic, olive oil, and oregano. The tomatoes' tangy acidity tenderizes the meat as it cooks, and it is served as a main course swimming in sauce. Whenever I cook this dish, I think of my mom, who would take me with her to the butcher to find the perfect cut of meat before we would run home to make it together. The smell and the aroma of the beef cooked in tomato sauce is a thing of beauty, just like my mamma.

Bring a large pot of water to a rolling boil over high heat.

Meanwhile, in a large deep sauté pan, sizzle the garlic in the olive oil over medium-low heat and cook until the garlic starts sizzling with little bubbles around it, 1 to 2 minutes. Add the tomato puree, a heavy pinch of salt, and a scrunch of pepper. Increase the heat to medium-high, add the oregano, and simmer for a minute or two before adding the beef. Submerge the meat in the simmering sauce and cook until soft and tender, about 10 minutes.

Once the water has reached a rolling boil, season with salt until the water tastes like a seasoned soup. Drop in the pasta and cook until al dente.

Remove the beef from the sauce and transfer to a platter. Transfer the candele to the sauce along with a splash (¼ cup) of the pasta cooking water and stir until they are drenched inside and out and the sauce has thickened.

Serve the pasta on the platter alongside the beef and garnish with an oregano sprig.

GORGEOUS TIP

Orange blossom water and rose water are sold in the baking or international aisles of supermarkets and big-box stores.

PASTIERA *di* TAGLIOLINI

PASTA CAKE

*Makes one 9- or 10-inch cake
(4 servings)*

---

*Total prep and cooking time:
1 hour 10 minutes*

Alternate pasta shape:
tagliatelle

4 tablespoons (½ stick) unsalted butter, plus more for greasing

¾ cup (150 grams/5¼ ounces) packed light brown sugar, plus more for sprinkling

5 large eggs

1 teaspoon vanilla extract

¼ teaspoon orange blossom water

¼ teaspoon rose water

1 teaspoon ground cinnamon

¼ cup candied orange peel, cut into ¼-inch dice

Grated zest of 1 lemon

Sea salt

Softened butter, for the pan

1 pound fresh tagliolini, homemade (see page 9) or store-bought

1 cup whole milk, well chilled

Powdered sugar, for dusting

Who says that pasta can't be a dessert? Or that a sweet pasta can't be a main course? For hundreds of years, pasta was dressed with sauces that would be considered sweet by modern standards, not unlike the classic spiced holiday sweets of Italy today. *Pastiera di tagliolini*, an Easter specialty of my Nonna Caterina's, is part of this tradition. Her ancient recipe combines long, thin pasta strands cut from Sfoglia all'Uovo (page 9) with a sweetened egg and candied fruit mixture that is then baked for the ultimate surprise. Each slice is a reminder that our ideas of what's "right" in terms of flavor were made to be challenged—and in fact, sometimes the most "inventive" dishes can go back to the ones that were most traditional.

Preheat the oven to 375°F.

Bring a large pot of water to a rolling boil over high heat.

Meanwhile, in a stand mixer fitted with the paddle attachment (or in a bowl with a hand mixer), cream the butter and brown sugar. Add the eggs, vanilla, orange blossom water, rose water, cinnamon, candied orange peel, and lemon zest and mix until smooth and silky.

Butter the bottom and sides of a 9- or 10-inch round pie plate or springform pan.

Once the water has reached a rolling boil, season with a pinch of salt. Drop in the tagliolini and cook until the pasta is tender, about 30 seconds.

Transfer the pasta to a bowl and pour the cold milk over it to cool it down and stop it from cooking.

Add the butter/egg mixture to the pasta/milk mixture and mix by hand. Transfer to the pie plate and smooth out with a spatula.

Bake until golden, about 1 hour. Serve cut into wedges dusted with powdered sugar.

ORECCHIETTE *con* POMODORO E CACIORICOTTA

ORECCHIETTE WITH
TOMATOES AND CHEESE

Serves 4

———

*Total prep and cooking time:
1 hour 20 minutes*

———

Alternate pasta shape:
ravioli

1 small onion, diced

Sea salt

¼ cup extra-virgin olive oil

1 pound grape tomatoes

6 to 8 fresh basil leaves, torn, plus
whole leaves for garnish

1 pound fresh orecchiette,
homemade (see page 30)
or store-bought

Cacioricotta, for grating

———

WATCH THIS RECIPE

My stepmother, Angela, and her mother, Michelina, were two of my kitchen role models when I was growing up. I loved learning the ingredients of their native Puglia, which Michelina would carefully pack in her luggage when she came to visit us in Rome for a few months each year. One of the treasures her luggage bore was cacioricotta, a cross between tangy cheese and ricotta. It's made with sheep and goat milk and has an almost herbal note due to the wild grasses the animals graze on. I love grating generous amounts of it over a quick and punchy tomato sauce perfumed with basil.

Bring a large pot of water to a rolling boil over high heat.

Meanwhile, in a large deep sauté pan, heat the onion and a pinch of salt in the olive oil over medium-low heat until the onion becomes slightly translucent and releases all of its flavor into the olive oil, 3 to 4 minutes. Add the grape tomatoes and torn basil, increase the heat to medium-high, and cook until the tomatoes burst, then soften, about 5 minutes. Season with salt.

Once the water has reached a rolling boil, season with salt until the water tastes like a seasoned soup. Drop in the orecchiette and cook until they float and are tender, about 3 minutes.

Transfer the pasta to the sauté pan and stir to combine, adding pasta cooking water as needed to loosen the sauce.

Serve with a generous flurry of cacioricotta on top and garnished with whole basil leaves.

CHAPTER FIVE

FALLING IN LOVE WITH AMERICA

Recipes for Comfort

People often ask me why I traded living in Italy for the United States. The answer is a mix of business and opportunity.

After five years in Rome followed by two in London, Brook and I went on a business trip to Florida. The weather was gorgeous, our marketing company was growing, and we immediately saw a future there. Florida has been our home ever since.

The move to America was exhilarating. I had so much energy, and it got my creative juices flowing, especially in the kitchen. Even though our company was thriving, great food remained my passion. A corporate lifestyle can be an emotionless monster that slowly eats away at the very core of your humanity (dramatic, maybe, but true). The key to solving this problem is to spend at least 50 percent of your time doing something that gives you pleasure and comfort. For me, that was cooking.

Life should not be wasted on stress, even when it's stressful. If you take a moment to do something for yourself, you will make different decisions. That is the culture of my family, and it works magic.

Around this time, I started a part-time YouTube cooking channel with a friend, where we cooked beautiful food and spread our humor and recipes through video. But editing was very hard, and finding an audience on such a massive platform was daunting. We eventually gave up YouTube and I threw myself back into work while I strategized how to accomplish my goals. I would not stop until I solved the problem. I had decided at a young age that I would bring my culture to the world, and it would be a happier place because of it. I decided that the time was now. No more waiting.

As life went on, our home in Florida became a regular rendezvous for local friends as well as family visiting from Italy. We had four or five visitors in the house at any given time of day, with the aroma of fresh food cooking from eight in the morning until eleven at night. I was alive. I suddenly realized that I had inadvertently molded my life into the direction I wanted it to go.

So, I gave my official resignation (or promotion?) to myself and started cooking full-time. I designed my dream kitchen with the Italian master craftsmen, Officine Gullo, from Florence, installed a dual-boiler espresso and cappuccino machine, and created an outdoor dining area under a beautiful oak tree. My home has never been the same since. Laughter, happiness, and energy permeates the whole house.

Since joining TikTok, and then Instagram, I have been working to make just-gorgeous recipes for you so that you, too, can experience the joy that cooking brings to me and to my loved ones. I am proof that with passion and hard work, your dreams can become reality, and I know that the comfort food in this chapter will nourish you every step of the way!

RADIATORI *al* FORNO

ITALIAN MAC AND CHEESE
BAKE

Serves 4

———

Total prep and cooking time:
45 minutes

———

Alternate pasta shapes:
lumache, maccheroni, ziti

Softened butter, for the baking dish

Sea salt

1 pound radiatori

1½ cups Béchamel (page 72)

1 pound Fontina cheese, cut into
½-inch pieces

4 ounces smoked provolone,
cut into ¼-inch pieces

100 grams/3½ ounces
(about 1¼ cups) finely grated
Parmigiano-Reggiano

Freshly ground black pepper

2 tablespoons unsalted butter,
sliced into pats

Mac and cheese might sound like a classic American dish, but some of the first published pasta recipes in Italy are actually very similar. Before tomatoes came to dominate pasta sauces in the nineteenth century, cheese was one of the most common ingredients in pasta dishes. So in spite of its name, this mac and cheese bake feels authentically Italian to me. When I created it, I channeled my Nonna Caterina, imagining how she would make such a dish in her truly unique style. She would bind Fontina and Parmigiano-Reggiano in a silky béchamel sauce and bake it with a ridged or textured pasta until the flavors were rich and united. When I served it for the first time, I knew I had nailed it when the kids fought over the last scoop.

Preheat the oven to 400°F. Butter a 9 × 13-inch baking dish with butter.

Bring a large pot of water to a rolling boil over high heat. Season with salt until the water tastes like a seasoned soup. Drop in the pasta and cook until al dente.

Transfer the pasta to the baking dish and stir in the béchamel, Fontina, provolone, three-quarters of the Parmigiano-Reggiano, and a scrunch of black pepper. Dot the top of the pasta with the butter pats, then dust with the remaining Parmigiano-Reggiano.

Bake until the Fontina melts and the Parmigiano-Reggiano starts to form a crust, about 20 minutes. Set aside to rest for 10 minutes before serving.

FINGER FOOD PASTA BAKE

Serves 10

———

*Total prep and cooking time:
55 minutes*

Sea salt

1 pound conchiglioni

2 cups Ricotta and Mushroom
Filling (page 29)

2½ ounces provolone, cut into
¼-inch cubes

120 grams/4¼ ounces
(about 1½ cups) finely grated
Parmigiano-Reggiano

1½ cups Béchamel (page 72)

I love pushing the limits of pasta. As an Italian, I grew up eating it served on plates and, in the case of the Frittata di Pasta (page 142), occasionally cut into wedges and eaten on the go. This pasta bake transforms pasta into finger food, perfect for a dinner party or as a fun snack or starter. To make it, I stuff *conchiglioni* (large shells) as I do for Conchiglioni al Forno con Pomodoro e Ricotta (page 150). But instead of ricotta and tomato, the filling is ricotta studded with gorgeous roasted mushrooms—the same filling I use for ravioli. The ricotta sizzles in the oven as mozzarella melts into all of the shells' gorgeous crevices, turning them into a love boat of flavor. I also make a variation that uses a ragù filling; see Finger Food Pasta with Ragù (opposite).

Preheat the oven to 400°F.

Bring a large pot of water to a rolling boil over high heat. Season with salt until the water tastes like a seasoned soup. Drop in the pasta and cook until very al dente (a little more than half the recommended cooking time); the pasta will finish cooking in the oven.

In a medium bowl, combine the ricotta and mushroom filling, the provolone, 90 grams/3 ounces of the Parmigiano-Reggiano and salt to taste. Spoon the mixture into the pasta shells, filling them loosely, and arrange them in a baking pan that can accommodate them snuggly. Spread the béchamel evenly over the top and dust with the remaining 30 grams/1¼ ounces Parmigiano-Reggiano.

Bake until golden, about 25 minutes.

Let the shells rest until they are lukewarm, about 10 minutes. Pick up with your fingers and devour with gusto.

Finger Food Pasta with Ragù

Use Ragù di Lady Caterina
or your own meat sauce.

Serves 10

Sea salt

1 pound conchiglioni

2½ cups Ragù di Lady Caterina (page 64)

12 ounces fresh mozzarella, torn into 1-inch pieces

2 tablespoons extra-virgin olive oil

60 grams/2 ounces (about ¾ cup) finely grated
Parmigiano-Reggiano

Fresh basil leaves, for garnish

Preheat the oven to 400°F.

Bring a large pot of water to a rolling boil over
high heat. Season with salt until the water tastes
like a seasoned soup. Drop in the pasta and
cook until very al dente (a little more than half
the recommended cooking time); the pasta will
finish cooking in the oven.

Spoon a thin layer of ragù on the bottom of a
baking pan large enough to fit the pasta snugly
in one layer. Spoon the remaining ragù into the
pasta shells, filling them loosely, and arrange
them in the pan. Sprinkle the mozzarella over
the shells, then drizzle with the olive oil. Dust
the top with the Parmigiano-Reggiano.

Bake until the mozzarella has melted, about
15 minutes.

Let the shells rest until they are lukewarm,
about 10 minutes, then garnish with the basil
leaves. Pick up with your fingers and devour
with gusto.

The DRUNKEN SALMON

PENNE WITH CREAMY
SALMON

Serves 4

Total prep and cooking time:
25 minutes

Alternate pasta shapes:
pennette, tonnarelli

Sea salt

1 pound penne

4 tablespoons (½ stick) unsalted
butter

300 grams/12 ounces smoked
salmon, cut into ½-inch-thick strips

3 tablespoons fresh lemon juice

1 cup whiskey, such as Scotch or
bourbon

1 cup heavy cream

Freshly ground black pepper

Roughly chopped fresh parsley
leaves, for garnish

The Drunken Salmon, while not seemingly Italian, spells pure comfort food for me. My mom really loves whiskey and would often cook with it, infusing her dishes with the amazing earthy flavor of the liquor. I sometimes cook with whiskey, too, like in this boozy homage to my mother. I spike the pan with it just as I would with vodka for *penne alla vodka* (see my version of this, Lady in Pink, page 218), transferring the woody notes of the whiskey to the cream. The dish feels wintery to me, and I imagine eating it by a fireplace while on a vacation in the Scottish Highlands, or anywhere chilly really. The smoked salmon soaks up the cream with its flavor and makes a gorgeous pink cloak for the penne.

Bring a large pot of water to a rolling boil over high heat. Season with salt until the water tastes like a seasoned soup. Drop in the pasta and cook until al dente.

Meanwhile, in a large deep sauté pan, heat the butter and smoked salmon over medium heat. Cook until the butter is frothy and golden, about 30 seconds. Stir in the lemon juice and whiskey. Increase the heat to medium-high and cook until the alcohol aroma dissipates and the liquid reduces by half, about 1½ minutes. Add the cream, season with salt and a scrunch of pepper, and simmer, stirring frequently, until the sauce thickens, about 5 minutes.

Transfer the pasta and a tablespoon or two of pasta cooking water to the sauté pan, stir, and simmer until the sauce coats the pasta.

Serve garnished with parsley.

CONCHIGLIETTE *ai* QUATTRO FORMAGGI

FOUR-CHEESE PASTA
WITH SMALL SHELLS

Serves 4

Total prep and cooking time:
45 minutes

Alternate pasta shapes:
radiatori, potato gnocchi

Sea salt

1 pound conchiglie

1 cup heavy cream

½ cup whole milk

4 tablespoons (½ stick)
unsalted butter

100 grams/3½ ounces
(about 1¼ cups) finely grated
Parmigiano-Reggiano

3 ounces Gruyère, grated

3 ounces Fontina, cut into
½-inch pieces

3 ounces Gorgonzola dolce, cut
into ½-inch pieces

Freshly ground black pepper

Freshly grated nutmeg

Coarsely chopped fresh parsley
leaves, for garnish

In Italy, *quattro formaggi* (four cheeses) is a term used for pizza toppings and pasta sauces. There are no set rules for the exact combination and proportions of cheeses, but I love watching melty Gruyère and Fontina disappear into simmering milk and heavy cream to envelop slightly funky Gorgonzola, then stirring in little shells that scoop up the creamy sauce. You can use any good melting cheeses you love—scamorza and provola are nice for this dish, too—but I recommend sticking with semi-creamy to dry cheeses and steering clear of mozzarella or cream cheese, which won't melt into the desired texture.

Bring a large pot of water to a rolling boil over high heat. Season with salt until the water tastes like a seasoned soup. Drop in the pasta and cook until al dente.

While the pasta is dancing in the water, in a large deep sauté pan, bring the cream and milk to a simmer over medium-high heat until it begins to thicken, about 5 minutes. Stir in the butter and the cheeses one at a time—Parmigiano-Reggiano, Gruyère, Fontina, and Gorgonzola—letting each melt before adding the next. Keep stirring until all the cheeses have melted into each other and simmer until the sauce thickens some more, about 2 minutes. Add a scrunch of pepper and a pinch of nutmeg.

Transfer the pasta to the sauté pan with 2 tablespoons of pasta cooking water, adding more as needed to loosen the sauce.

Serve garnished with parsley leaves.

RISOTTO *al* POMODORO E MOZZARELLA

TOMATO AND MOZZARELLA
RISOTTO

Serves 4

Total prep and cooking time:
1 hour

6 tablespoons extra-virgin olive oil

1 shallot, diced

Sea salt

2½ cups rice (Carnaroli or Arborio)

1½ cups tomato sauce

1 cup dry white wine

4 cups Homemade Vegetable Broth
(page 115) or store-bought

60 grams/2 ounces (about ¾ cup)
finely grated Parmigiano-Reggiano,
plus more for dusting

8 ounces fresh mozzarella, cut into
½-inch pieces

Fresh basil leaves, for garnish

For Italians, risotto's ancestral homeland is in the north of Italy, but that's not to say you won't find it all over the country. We make it in Southern Italy, too, forming it into croquettes called *supplì* in Rome and *arancine* in Sicily. To me, risotto can be anything I want it to be, and in this dish it's the vehicle for two of my favorite ingredients—tomato and mozzarella—the supreme comfort ingredients that remind me of home. This simple duo teams up to make a risotto that has an acidic tang tamed by milky mozzarella, which melts beautifully to create the most complementary masterpiece. It reminds me of Gnocchi alla Sorrentina (page 56), another dish that promises a gooey melted cheese with every bite. When crowned with basil, this gorgeous dish reaches an amazing peak of Italian flavor.

In a large saucepan, heat 4 tablespoons of the olive oil, the shallot, and a heavy pinch of salt over medium-low heat until the shallot becomes slightly translucent and releases all of its flavor into the olive oil, 3 to 4 minutes. Increase the heat to medium-high, then pour in the rice and stir to coat it in the oil. Continue stirring until the rice is lightly toasted and turns translucent, a couple of minutes. Add the tomato sauce and stir until it is absorbed. Add the wine and stir until the alcohol aroma dissipates and the liquid reduces by half, about 1½ minutes. Add vegetable broth to cover the rice and cook, stirring constantly to prevent the rice from sticking to the pan, until the broth has been absorbed, a few minutes. Add more broth and cook, stirring constantly, until it has been absorbed, about 4 minutes longer. Add another ½ cup broth, stirring constantly, until it has been absorbed, about 10 minutes. If you need more liquid for cooking the rice, add more as needed. The rice is done when it is al dente. You may not need all the broth.

Stir in the remaining 2 tablespoons of olive oil. Remove from the heat and fold in the Parmigiano-Reggiano, then stir in the mozzarella until it melts. Serve garnished with basil leaves and dusted with Parmigiano-Reggiano.

ORECCHIETTE *con* CIME *di* RAPA E SALSICCIA

ORECCHIETTE
WITH BROCCOLI RABE
AND SAUSAGE

Serves 4

Total prep and cooking time:
40 minutes

Alternate pasta shape:
fresh cavatelli

1 garlic clove, minced

1 fresh chili pepper (I like cayenne
and Calabrian chilis), sliced into
⅛-inch-thick rounds

¼ cup extra-virgin olive oil

2 (8-ounce) sweet Italian sausage
links, casings removed

½ cup dry white wine

Sea salt

1 pound broccoli rabe, tough stems
trimmed, cut into 1-inch pieces,
or 1 small head broccoli, florets
separated and stalks cut into 1-inch
pieces

1 pound fresh orecchiette,
homemade (see page 30) or
store-bought

If there's a vegetable I cannot and will not live without it has to be broccoli rabe. It was a yearly tradition to celebrate this green wonder at a *sagra*, or local festival, near Naples. When I was a kid, I would eagerly await this fair, as it meant there would be endless fried broccoli rabe available. Walking around town holding a panino with sausage and broccoli rabe was as delightful and exciting to me as going on the merry-go-rounds or roller coaster rides that flooded the sagra. Needless to say, when my Pugliese stepmother, Angela, introduced me to this dish, it quickly became one of my favorites.

Bring a large pot of water to a rolling boil over high heat.

While the water is coming to a boil, in a large deep sauté pan, heat the garlic and chili pepper in the olive oil over medium-low heat until they start sizzling with little bubbles around them, 1 to 2 minutes. Add the sausage and cook, using the back of a spoon to break it into small pieces, just until it begins to brown, about 3 minutes. Add the wine and cook until the alcohol aroma dissipates and the liquid reduces by half, about 1½ minutes.

Once the water has reached a rolling boil, season with a pinch of salt. Add the broccoli rabe and cook until tender, about 2 minutes. Then drain, keeping the water boiling for cooking the orecchiette. Add the broccoli rabe to the sausage mixture.

Season the boiling water with salt until it tastes like a seasoned soup. Drop the orecchiette into the water and cook until they float and are tender, about 3 minutes.

Transfer the pasta and 2 tablespoons of pasta cooking water to the sauté pan and stir to combine.

Serve.

VEGAN LADY *of the* NIGHT

GLUTEN-FREE FARFALLE
WITH TOMATO, EGGPLANT,
OLIVES, AND CAPERS

Serves 4

———

*Total prep and cooking time:
1 hour 25 minutes*

———

Alternate pasta shapes:
gluten-free penne, ziti, or fusilli

3 cups cubed (½-inch) eggplant
(about 1 large eggplant)

2 garlic cloves, minced

½ cup extra-virgin olive oil

Sea salt

1 pound grape tomatoes, halved

½ cup olives (I like Gaeta or
Kalamata)

2 tablespoons capers
(rinsed and soaked if salt-packed,
drained if in brine)

250 grams/9 ounces canned
whole peeled tomatoes, crushed by
hand (see page 58)

1 pound gluten-free farfalle

Fresh basil leaves, for garnish

Really any pasta dish in this book can be prepared with gluten-free pasta. But the Vegan Lady of the Night was specifically born with gluten-free roots. My husband, Brook, has a mild gluten intolerance and he absolutely loves the flavors of summertime. I created this dish for him and I prepared it for him with all the love and heat of summer. In addition to being inspired by gluten-free pasta, Vegan Lady of the Night also draws its flavors from Puttanesca (page 71), omitting the anchovies or tuna, and enriches it with eggplant, the quintessential summer ingredient in the south of Italy. The sauce is just incredible with its eggplant, olives, and capers mingling in tomatoes, a vegan variation on a classic that celebrates the greatest hits of seasonal Southern Italian flavors.

Place the eggplant in a colander and sprinkle all over with abundant salt. Set aside to drain, weighted down, for 1 hour. Rinse, then pat dry with paper towels.

Bring a large pot of water to a rolling boil over high heat.

Meanwhile, in a large deep sauté pan, sizzle the garlic in the olive oil over low heat until bubbles form around it, 1 to 2 minutes. Add the eggplant, increase the heat to medium, and shower it with some salt. Stir, adding water as needed to cook the eggplant until tender, about 8 minutes. Add the grape tomatoes, increase the heat to medium-high, season with salt, and cook until the tomatoes soften, about 5 minutes. Stir in the olives and capers. Pour in the canned tomatoes, season with salt, and cook until the sauce has thickened and the tomatoes have lost their raw flavor, about 8 minutes.

Once the water has reached a rolling boil, season with salt until the water tastes like a seasoned soup. Drop in the pasta and cook until al dente.

Add the pasta to the sauté pan along with a few spoonfuls of the tears of the gods. Simmer briefly to bring the flavors together and thicken the sauce. Serve garnished with basil leaves.

PASTA *al* BAFFO

RIGATONI WITH TOMATO,
CREAM, AND PROSCIUTTO

Serves 4

———

Total prep and cooking time:
25 minutes

———

Alternate pasta shapes:
penne, ziti

1 small white onion, diced

½ cup extra-virgin olive oil

Sea salt

6 slices (about 5 ounces)
thinly sliced Prosciutto di Parma,
cut into ¼-inch ribbons

1 (14.5-ounce) can whole
peeled tomatoes, crushed by
hand (see page 58)

1 cup heavy cream

1 pound rigatoni

1 teaspoon chili flakes, or to taste,
plus more for garnish

Roughly chopped fresh parsley
leaves, for garnish

Pasta al baffo (literally, "mustache pasta") is a delicious and extremely quick pasta dish in which a tomato cream sauce is perfumed by a bit of prosciutto crudo (cured ham) or the cured meat of your desire. The dish's name derives from the Italian saying *leccarsi I baffi*, or to lick one's mustache in anticipation of eating something delicious. It doesn't have a particular regional identity like Carbonara (page 39), which is extremely Roman, but instead is made in rough and ready trattorias all over the country. There are many variations of *pasta al baffo*, including swapping out the prosciutto for pancetta, ham, or speck (smoked cured ham). You can add peas, sausage, or any other vegetable or meat you wish, or leave out the pork altogether for a vegetarian version.

Bring a large pot of water to a rolling boil over high heat.

Meanwhile, in a large deep sauté pan, sizzle the onion in the olive oil, showering it with a pinch of salt, over medium-low heat until it becomes slightly translucent and releases all of its flavor into the olive oil, 3 to 4 minutes. Add the prosciutto and sizzle for about 30 seconds to infuse the oil. Add the tomatoes, season with salt, and bring to a simmer over medium-high heat, cooking until the tomatoes lose their raw flavor, about 6 minutes. Pour in the cream to bring it all together. Simmer, stirring frequently, until the sauce has thickened, about 5 minutes.

Once the water has reached a rolling boil, season with salt until the water tastes like a seasoned soup. Drop in the pasta and cook until al dente.

Transfer the pasta to the sauté pan along with a couple of tablespoons of the tears of the gods and stir vigorously with the passion of a lover until the pasta is enveloped in the velvety sauce. Add a rainfall of chili flakes to spice up your life.

Serve garnished with more chili flakes and parsley sprinkled on top.

FETTUCCINE *alle* ZUCCHINE

FETTUCCINE
WITH ZUCCHINI

Serves 4

Total prep and cooking time:
30 minutes

Alternate pasta shape:
mezze maniche

1 small white onion, diced

Sea salt

¼ cup extra-virgin olive oil

¾ pound zucchini, cut into
¼-inch-thick rounds

2 sprigs fresh thyme

1 cup dry white wine

1 pound fresh fettuccine,
homemade (see page 9) or
store-bought

1 tablespoon aged balsamic vinegar
(I like 12-year aged Aceto Balsamico
Tradizionale di Modena)

60 grams/2 ounces (about ¾ cup)
finely grated Pecorino Romano

60 grams/2 ounces (about ¾ cup)
finely grated Parmigiano-Reggiano,
plus more for dusting

This dish is my mom's favorite and I adore cooking it for my family. She tosses soft simmered zucchini with fresh zucchini and grated cheeses, finishing the dish with a surprising but welcome addition: aged balsamic vinegar. The thick, tart, and slightly sweet vinegar mingles with the pasta strands and their savory sauce for a flavor that is just gorgeous. My favorite time to cook with zucchini is at the beginning of their season in early summer, when they are sweet and tender with barely any seeds. I grow my own zucchini and they are some of the easiest, lowest maintenance plants to grow. I love cooking them until tender, and then blending a portion to create a lovely contrast between the al dente zucchini pieces and the creamy zucchini puree.

Bring a large pot of water to a rolling boil over high heat.

Meanwhile, in a large deep sauté pan, sizzle the onion and a pinch of salt in the olive oil over medium-low heat until the onion becomes slightly translucent and releases all of its flavors into the olive oil, 3 to 4 minutes. Add the zucchini and season with salt. Increase the heat to medium-high, add the thyme, and cook until fragrant, about 1 minute, then add the wine and cook until the alcohol aroma has evaporated and the liquid has reduced by half, about 1½ minutes. Continue cooking until the zucchini are soft and gorgeous, about 6 minutes, adding a splash (¼ cup) of water as needed to keep the pan moist. Discard the sprigs of thyme.

Once the water has reached a rolling boil, season with salt until the water tastes like a seasoned soup. Drop in the pasta and cook until the fettuccine are tender, 1 to 2 minutes.

Add the fettuccine to the sauté pan with the zucchini. Remove from the heat and stir in the balsamic vinegar, followed by the Pecorino Romano and Parmigiano-Reggiano. Toss with the passion of an Italian until the sauce envelops the pasta strands, adding a bit of pasta cooking water as needed to keep the sauce luscious. Serve dusted with some Parmigiano-Reggiano.

MINESTRA *di* SPAGHETTI

CREAMY SPAGHETTI
SOUP

Serves 4

Total prep and cooking time:
35 minutes

Alternate pasta shapes:
spaghettoni, candele, ziti lunghi

1 garlic clove, peeled

¼ cup extra-virgin olive oil, plus
more for drizzling

3 or 4 fresh basil leaves, torn, plus
whole leaves for garnish

1 (28-ounce) can tomato puree

Sea salt

1 pound spaghetti, broken into
3-inch pieces

Finely grated Parmigiano-Reggiano,
for dusting

I had the pleasure of cooking with my dear friend and Michelin-starred chef Peppe Guida when I was recently in Italy. Eating this dish with him as we sat in his gardens overlooking the Gulf of Naples has now become a cherished memory of mine. It's made with pure love, just like you are. You will not find many recipes in Italy that call for breaking spaghetti, so this is an exception to the usual way of doing things. Peppe's mother made this soup for him while he was growing up, and he continues to pass the tradition on. It has now become a favorite in my own family.

In a medium pot, bring 3 cups water to a rolling boil over high heat.

In a large pot, cook the garlic in the olive oil over medium-low heat until it starts sizzling with little bubbles around it, 1 to 2 minutes. Increase the heat to medium and add the basil leaves, sizzling until fragrant, about 15 seconds. Add the tomato puree and a heavy pinch of salt. Increase the heat to medium-high and stir in the spaghetti. Add the simmering water a splash (¼ cup) at a time as needed to cook the pasta until it is al dente. Remove and discard the garlic.

Serve garnished with basil leaves and dusted with Parmigiano-Reggiano. Finish with a drizzle of olive oil.

FUSILLI *all'*ORTOLANA

🌿

SEASONAL GARDEN PASTA

Serves 4

———

Total prep and cooking time:
45 minutes

———

Alternate pasta shape:
fusilloni

1 small red onion, diced

1 carrot, diced

1 celery stalk, diced

Sea salt

½ cup extra-virgin olive oil

1 red bell pepper, and cut into
½-inch-wide strips

1 yellow bell pepper, and cut into
½-inch-wide strips

2 small zucchini, cut into
½-inch-wide strips

2 cups jarred Pomodori del
Piennolo del Vesuvio tomatoes or
230 grams/8 ounces grape
tomatoes, halved

1 small eggplant, cut into ½-inch-
wide × 3-inch-long strips

1 pound fusilli

6 to 8 fresh basil leaves, torn, plus
more leaves for garnish

This vegetarian pasta takes me back to my nonna's garden. Each day during summer holidays, my brother, Agostino, and I would wake up early to pick Nonna's ripe peppers, eggplants, tomatoes, and zucchini, which felt warm beneath our fingertips after weeks of maturing under the blazing Neapolitan sun. These memories bring the same joy I have picking vegetables with my own children in our garden under the Florida sunshine. What I love most about this dish—aside from the nostalgia it brings flooding back—is that it is so flexible. You can make it your own with what's in season no matter where you are and any time of the year, even in the winter, substituting winter squashes and bitter greens for the summery medley below. Cook the vegetables in stages so they all finish cooking at the same time—knowing how to time this perfectly comes with practice, but one bite of this dish and I know you'll be hooked and up for the challenge.

Bring a large pot of water to a rolling boil over high heat.

Meanwhile, in a large deep sauté pan, sizzle the onion, carrot, celery, and a heavy pinch of salt in the olive oil over low heat and cook until soft, about 15 minutes. Add the bell peppers, zucchini, and a splash (¼ cup) of water, season with salt, and cook until they begin to soften, about 5 minutes. Add the tomatoes and eggplant and another splash of water, season with salt once again, and bring to a simmer. Reduce the heat to low, cover, and cook until the vegetables are tender, about 10 minutes. Add a bit of water to prevent sticking as needed.

Once the water has reached a rolling boil, season with salt until the water tastes like a seasoned soup. Drop in the pasta and cook until al dente.

Transfer the pasta to the sauté pan. Stir in the basil along with a few spoonfuls of pasta cooking water and mix gently as the sauce thickens slightly over the heat to coat the pasta. Serve garnished with fresh basil leaves.

CANNELLONI

Sauce

3 tablespoons extra-virgin olive oil

1 garlic clove, minced

6 fresh basil leaves, torn

1 (14.5-ounce) can whole peeled
tomatoes

Sea salt

Filling

½ pound fresh spinach or 1 cup
frozen cooked spinach, thawed

2 cups Homemade Ricotta
(page 186) or store-bought fresh
ricotta (I like sheep's milk)

60 grams/2 ounces (about ¾ cup)
finely grated Parmigiano-Reggiano

1 large egg

½ teaspoon freshly grated nutmeg

Freshly ground black pepper

Sea salt

Cannelloni are a labor of love that start by rolling fresh pasta sheets (Sfoglio all'Uovo, page 9) and mixing fresh ricotta with cooked spinach and seasonings. The pasta is rolled around the filling into tubes, then baked with cheese that melts into a gorgeous crust. Cannelloni reminds me of a lasagna, but it's a little less work. Still, this isn't something I can pull together in an hour, so I save it for a weekend or special occasion when I can recruit a few extra sets of hands to help me assemble.

Preheat the oven to 350°F.

Make the sauce: In a large sauté pan, heat the olive oil and garlic over medium-low heat until the garlic starts sizzling with little bubbles around it, 1 to 2 minutes. Add the basil and sizzle until fragrant, about 15 seconds. Add the tomatoes, season with salt, increase the heat to medium, and cook just until the tomatoes lose their acidic edge, 5 to 6 minutes.

Make the filling: Bring a large pot of water to a rolling boil over high heat. Working in batches, blanch the fresh spinach until the stems become tender, about 2 minutes. Let cool, then wrap it in cheesecloth or a kitchen towel and squeeze out any liquid over the sink. Finely chop.

In a food processor, combine the ricotta, Parmigiano-Reggiano, egg, the nutmeg, and a scrunch of pepper and blend until very smooth, about 30 seconds. Fold in the spinach. (Alternatively, mix the ingredients together vigorously by hand in a medium bowl.) Season with salt to taste.

Transfer the mixture to a pastry bag with a wide tip or to a sturdy plastic bag with one corner trimmed off.

Prepare the cannelloni: Ladle about half of the tomato sauce into the bottom of a 9 × 13-inch baking dish.

Lay the pasta sheets (around 12) on a clean, dry work surface. Pipe equal amounts of the ricotta mixture along the middle of each piece of pasta, then roll into a medium tight tube and transfer to the baking dish.

Ladle the remaining tomato sauce over the filled tubes, then drape the provolone slices evenly over the top. Sprinkle with the Parmigiano-Reggiano.

Bake until the pasta is cooked and the cheese is gorgeously melted, about 25 minutes.

Set aside for 10 minutes to set before serving. The cannelloni need time to rest before traveling to your plate. Serve with any extra sauce from the pan ladled on top and garnish with fresh basil leaves.

Cannelloni

1 pound Sfoglia all'Uovo (page 9) or store-bought fresh pasta sheets, cut into 6 × 8-inch pieces

12 thin slices (about 8 ounces) provolone

60 grams/2 ounces (about ¾ cup) finely grated Parmigiano-Reggiano

Fresh basil leaves, for garnish

GORGEOUS TIP

In Italy, the ricotta is thick and sliceable due to the richness of the milk and the techniques used by dairy farms. If your ricotta is loose or liquidy, drain it in a colander lined with a double thickness of cheesecloth and gently squeeze out any excess moisture.

recipe continues

Homemade Ricotta

Let's be honest. This is not technically ricotta because it is made with fresh dairy instead of cooked whey. But it's pretty close in flavor, and unless you have an incredible Italian food store near you, it will be as good—if not better!—than anything store-bought. You'll need a cheesecloth, a sieve, and a thermometer before you get started. You can use the liquid left behind when you drain the ricotta to soften bread crumbs for Polpettine (page 76).

Makes 2 cups

6 cups whole milk

2 cups heavy cream

1 teaspoon sea salt

¼ cup plus 2 tablespoons lemon juice

In a medium pot, heat the milk and cream over medium heat, stirring in the salt as the mixture warms. Once the mixture reaches 190°F, remove from the heat and drizzle in the lemon juice. Stir until the mixture begins to visibly curdle, then allow it to sit undisturbed for 10 minutes.

Line a colander with a cheesecloth folded over a few times. Set it above a pot or bowl for collecting the excess liquid. Pour in the ricotta mixture and allow it to drain for 1 hour. Gather the cheesecloth and gently squeeze out any excess liquid. The ricotta will keep for up to 3 days in the refrigerator.

PACCHERI *con* CARCIOFI E POMODORINI

PACCHERI WITH ARTICHOKE
AND TOMATO

Serves 4

———

Total prep and cooking time:
40 minutes

———

Alternate pasta shapes:
rigatoni, fettuccine

¼ cup extra-virgin olive oil

2 garlic cloves, peeled

6 globe artichokes, trimmed
(see How to Trim Artichokes,
opposite) and cut into ¼-inch-thick
wedges, chokes removed

Sea salt and freshly ground
black pepper

1 cup dry white wine

¾ pound cherry tomatoes, halved

1 pound paccheri

Freshly grated Pecorino Romano,
for dusting (optional)

When I think of my friend Leo, I can taste this artichoke and cherry tomato pasta dish. Leo is a proud Roman who owns a trattoria by the Vatican. He has been there since he was barely a teenager, and I visit his restaurant every time I'm in Rome. I love when Leo walks over to my table and brings me a little house wine to enhance my experience. He sits down and we have a good chat, laughing at each other's latest adventures. I re-create this earthy pasta dish in the winter, when artichokes are in season, whenever I want a little taste of home.

Bring a large pot of water to a rolling boil over high heat.

Meanwhile, in a large deep sauté pan, heat the olive oil and garlic over medium-low heat until the garlic starts sizzling with little bubbles around it, 1 to 2 minutes. Increase the heat to medium and add the artichoke pieces. Season with a heavy pinch of salt and a scrunch of pepper. Add the wine and cook until the artichokes just begin to soften, about 15 minutes, adding a splash of water as needed to keep the artichokes cooking in a small amount of liquid. Add the tomatoes and season with salt. Cook until they begin to melt into the sauce, about 8 minutes longer.

Once the water has reached a rolling boil, season with salt until the water tastes like a seasoned soup. Drop in the pasta and cook until al dente.

Transfer the paccheri to the sauté pan with a splash of pasta cooking water and swirl until the paccheri are coated inside and out and the sauce is nice and juicy.

Serve dusted with Pecorino Romano (if using).

HOW TO TRIM ARTICHOKES

Fill a large bowl with cold water. Halve a lemon, squeeze the juice into the water, and drop the halves into the bowl. The lemon water will keep your artichokes from turning brown. Snap off the outer leaves of each artichoke until you reach the tender, lighter-colored inner heart. If your artichokes have stems, cut the stem off, leaving about 1 inch attached to the base. Using a small knife, peel off the outer layer from the stem until you reach the inner flesh. Place the stem in the lemon water. Trim away the tough, outer skin from the base of the artichoke and any tough bits from the tips of the artichoke leaves. Drop in the lemon water until ready to use.

GORGEOUS TIP

The success of this recipe rests on managing the moisture in the pan as the artichokes slowly cook. Watch them as they cook and let them tell you how often they need a splash of liquid to make them tender.

RAVIOLI BURRO E SALVIA

RICOTTA AND
SPINACH RAVIOLI WITH
BUTTER AND SAGE

Serves 4

———

*Total prep and cooking time:
1 hour 20 minutes*

———

Alternate pasta shape:
potato gnocchi

4 tablespoons (½ stick)
unsalted butter

Sea salt

8 to 10 fresh sage leaves

1¼ pounds Ravioli (page 26)
or store-bought fresh ravioli

Freshly grated
Parmigiano-Reggiano, for
dusting (optional)

Ricotta is one of my most favorite ingredients. I love eating it in so many ways—on toast with drizzled chestnut honey and a scrunch of black pepper, sweetened with sugar and piped into a Sicilian *cannolo*, or folded with spinach and used to fill ravioli. In all cases, I love when ricotta is the star, complemented rather than overpowered by the other ingredients. That's why my go-to sauce for ravioli is sage-infused butter. The fragrant sage and the rich, slightly sweet butter conspire to prop up the ricotta's fresh milk flavors. To make ravioli from scratch, you will need to roll sfoglia all'uovo and then fill and shape the ravioli according to the instructions on page 28. For a quick, 20-minute version, use store-bought ravioli instead.

Bring a large pot of water to a rolling boil over high heat.

Meanwhile, in a large deep sauté pan, combine the butter, a heavy pinch of salt, and the sage over medium heat. Cook until the butter is frothy and golden, about 30 seconds. Remove from the heat.

Once the water has reached a rolling boil, season with salt until the water tastes like a seasoned soup. Drop in the ravioli and cook until they float and are tender, 2½ to 3 minutes.

Return the sauté pan to medium heat. Carefully transfer the ravioli to the pan using a spider or slotted spoon. Swirl the ravioli in the pan to coat with the butter.

Serve with the butter and sage drizzled on top, and dusted with Parmigiano-Reggiano (if using).

Variations

Simple meat and tomato sauces will also complement the ricotta filling of the ravioli.

RAVIOLI WITH RAGÙ:
In a large sauté pan, heat 2 cups of Lady Caterina's Ragù (page 64) over medium heat. After cooking the ravioli, add it to the pan with a couple of tablespoons of pasta water and swirl to coat. Serve with Parmigiano-Reggiano dusted on top.

RAVIOLI WITH TOMATO SAUCE:
In a large sauté pan, heat 2 cups Fresh Tomato Sauce (page 155) over medium heat. After cooking the ravioli, add it to the pan with a couple of tablespoons of pasta water and swirl to coat. Serve garnished with fresh basil leaves and dusted with Parmigiano-Reggiano (if using).

PASTA *al* SUGO

SPAGHETTI WITH A
15-MINUTE TOMATO SAUCE

Serves 4

———

Total prep and cooking time:
25 minutes

———

Alternate pasta shapes:
Any pasta shape will work with this
gorgeous recipe.

2 garlic cloves, minced practically
to a paste

¼ cup extra-virgin olive oil

6 to 8 fresh basil leaves, torn, plus
whole leaves for garnish

1 (28-ounce) can whole peeled
tomatoes, crushed by hand
(see page 58)

Sea salt

1 pound spaghetti

Freshly grated Pecorino Romano or
Parmigiano-Reggiano, for dusting
(optional)

———

WATCH THIS RECIPE

Pasta al sugo is the essence of life. Every Italian dreams of this dish, which is as simple and quick as it is gorgeous. When the garlic and basil infuse the tomatoes, it creates an unstoppable force of nature (just like you are). In Italy, this is one of our most beloved dishes, and we make it any time we want to feel caressed by the classic flavors of home. It's so fundamental to Italians that we don't even call it "pasta with tomato," it's simply "pasta with sauce." The tomato is such a star, its presence is implied.

Due to this dish's simplicity, you really have to use the best canned tomatoes you can find. There is a huge range of different ones out there, and many of them put "Made in Italy" on the label as shorthand for quality. But the only way to know if a canned tomato is truly great is to taste and feel it. Open the can, touch the tomatoes: Do they have tough bits? Do you see any green, unripened parts? Taste a spoonful: Are they too acidic? These are all red flags for me. I want a juicy, ripe-tasting tomato that contains a perfect balance of acidity and sweetness. Long story short: If it doesn't taste good from the can, it won't taste good on the pasta. Search out some special *pomodori* and your palate (and pasta!) will thank you!

Bring a large pot of water to a rolling boil over high heat.

Meanwhile, in a large deep sauté pan, heat the garlic and olive oil over medium-low heat until the garlic starts sizzling with little bubbles around it, 1 to 2 minutes. Add the basil and sizzle until fragrant, about 10 seconds, then add the tomatoes and stir in salt to taste. Increase the heat to medium-high and let the tomato sauce bubble vigorously until the tomatoes lose their raw flavor, about 7 minutes.

Once the water has reached a rolling boil, season with salt until the water tastes like a seasoned soup. Drop in the pasta and cook until very al dente (a little more than half the recommended cooking time).

Transfer the pasta to the sauté pan along with a ladle (½ cup) of pasta cooking water and cook, stirring, until the pasta is al dente. Check frequently to see when the pasta is done and add more pasta cooking water as needed to finish cooking the pasta and keep the sauce loose.

Serve topped with Pecorino Romano (if using) and fresh basil leaves.

GORGEOUS TIP

Cook this pasta dish in a cast-iron skillet for maximum deadliness.

The ASSASSIN'S SPAGHETTI

PAN-FRIED SPICY
SPAGHETTI

Serves 4

Total prep and cooking time:
30 minutes

Alternate pasta shape:
spaghettoni

¼ cup tomato paste

Sea salt

2 garlic cloves, minced

1 tablespoon Calabrian chili flakes,
or to taste

¼ cup extra-virgin olive oil

1 (14.5-ounce) can whole peeled
tomatoes, crushed by hand
(see page 58)

1 pound spaghetti

Whole fresh long red chili peppers
(I like cayenne varieties like
Pinocchio's nose), for garnish

WATCH THIS RECIPE

This is a very famous dish from Puglia, and the recipe is based on an *almost* true story. Legend has it that a drunk cook at a restaurant in Bari was distracted by a beautiful woman passing by and put uncooked spaghetti directly into his cast iron pan of simmering tomato sauce that he had overloaded with too much garlic and chili peppers. Once the spaghetti absorbed the sauce, it began to burn on the bottom of the pan, alerting the cook with its spicy and smoky aromas. He tried to save the dish from disaster by making a tomato paste broth and slowly adding it to the pan, *risottata*-style (see page xxiii), inventing something totally unique. The pasta became one with the chili peppers and the tomatoes, and it was so beautifully flawed and perfect that he decided to serve it to a guest who, upon eating it, was so overwhelmed by the spice he shouted, "What are you trying to do—kill me?!" Thus, the Assassin's Spaghetti was born. Serve this to spice up your life.

In a medium pot, bring 6 cups water to a rolling boil over high heat. Stir in the tomato paste until it dissolves to create a tomato broth. If necessary, season it with salt until it tastes like a seasoned soup and keep the tomato broth warm over a very low heat.

Meanwhile, in a large deep sauté pan, sizzle the garlic and chili flakes in the olive oil over low heat. Add the tomatoes and a heavy pinch of salt. Increase the heat to medium high and add the uncooked spaghetti. Ladle in the tomato broth to keep the spaghetti just barely submerged, adding more as needed. Let the pasta cook until it sticks to the bottom of the pan and starts to burn slightly. Toss briefly and add a splash (¼ cup) tomato broth to the pasta. Cook until al dente, allowing the pasta to completely absorb the liquid. Add ¼ cup tomato broth at a time as needed to finish cooking the pasta.

Serve garnished with fresh chili peppers.

TONNARELLI *con* ORATA E LIMONE

FRESH PASTA WITH
GILT-HEAD BREAM
AND LEMON

Serves 4

Total prep and cooking time:
25 minutes

Alternate pasta shapes:
fresh tagliolini, tagliatelle, or spaghetti

3 tablespoons extra-virgin olive oil

1 garlic clove, minced

1 tablespoon roughly chopped
fresh parsley leaves, plus more for
garnish

1 pound gilt-head bream fillet, cut
into 1-inch pieces

Sea salt

1 pound homemade tonnarelli
(see page 14) or store-bought fresh
spaghetti alla chitarra

Zest and juice (about
3 tablespoons) of 1 lemon

Orata, or gilt-head bream, is a sweet and mild fish that swims in the waters of the Tyrrhenian Sea near Rome and Naples. Its soft texture and delicate flavor beg for a splash of lemon to make it just perfect. This is the type of fish that you might order whole at a seaside restaurant in Italy, but it also makes a beautiful partner for pasta, and that's exactly what I want to eat on a hot day on the Amalfi Coast as I gaze out over the water. The great news is you can enjoy this dish year-round, no matter where you are. If you don't have a gilt-head bream source, you can use sea bass or sea bream in its place. The fish will flake delicately when the pasta is mixed in, making the impression of a sort of light fish ragù.

Bring a large pot of water to a rolling boil over high heat.

Separately, while the water reaches a rolling boil, heat the oil, garlic, and parsley in a large pan over medium-low heat until they start sizzling with little bubbles around them, 1 to 2 minutes. Increase the heat to medium, add the fish and a flurry of salt, and cook until the fish is just cooked through, a few minutes, adding a bit of water if needed to keep the pan moist.

When the water in the pasta pot has reached a rolling boil, season with salt until it tastes like a seasoned soup. Add the pasta and cook until the tonnarelli are tender, 2 to 2½ minutes.

Add the tonnarelli, half the lemon zest, another splash of pasta cooking water, and the lemon juice to the pan and toss with the passion of an Italian until the pasta strands and fish are fully mingled.

Serve with parsley and the remaining lemon zest sprinkled on top.

TONNARELLI *alla* LEO

TONNARELLI
WITH ANCHOVIES AND
PECORINO ROMANO

Serves 4

Total prep and cooking time:
15 minutes

Alternate pasta shapes
spaghetti, linguine

2 tablespoons extra-virgin olive oil

2 garlic cloves, minced

5 oil-packed anchovy fillets,
drained

230 grams/8 ounces cherry
tomatoes, halved

Sea salt

1 sprig fresh oregano, picked

1 pound homemade tonnarelli
(see page 14)

60 grams/2 ounces (about ¾ cup)
finely grated Pecorino Romano

Growing up by the Vatican, it was impossible not to strike a friendship with Leo and Fabio, the owners of Osteria dei Pontefici, a family-run tavern in the shadow of the *cupolone* (St. Peter's dome). It was a tiny restaurant at first and it could barely host visitors other than their family members! Every time I go back home I visit and spend a whole week recharging on the amazing fresh dishes they prepare for me. Last time I was there I told Leo I was writing a cookbook, so we developed this recipe together for you all.

In a large deep sauté pan, heat the olive oil and garlic over medium-low heat until bubbles start sizzling around the garlic, 1 to 2 minutes. Add the anchovies and cook until they melt into the oil, about 2 minutes. Add the tomatoes, season with salt and oregano, and cook until the tomatoes begin to soften, about 5 minutes.

Meanwhile, bring a large pot of water to a rolling boil over high heat. When the water has reached a rolling boil, season with salt until the water tastes like a seasoned soup. Add the pasta and cook until the tonnarelli are tender, 2 to 2½ minutes.

Transfer the pasta to the sauté pan with a ladle (½ cup) of the tears of the gods. Stir in the pecorino energetically until the sauce is creamy and serve.

CHAPTER SIX

THE PASTA RENAISSANCE

—

Creative Dishes

When I reflect on my journey to becoming the Pasta Queen, I often think about Italian Renaissance painters.

At first, they are students and apprentices, humbly learning their brush strokes and techniques from their master. Then they strike out on their own, painting in the style they have learned in their master's studio. With time and practice, they build their confidence, give birth to their own style, and become masters—and therefore teachers—themselves. My masters' workshops were the kitchens of my Nonna Caterina and my aunts Pina and Stella, where I made my first pasta dough, sizzled my first garlic clove, and ladled hot pasta cooking water into my first sauce.

Between Nonna Caterina and my aunties, I learned all the basics of Italian cooking, built an appreciation for the classics, and took no shortcuts as I cooked alongside them, eager to make them proud. When I left Italy for London, I cooked what I knew, like a young Renaissance painter, leaning on the lessons I had absorbed from my masters and replicating the recipes of my childhood. As I grew as a person, becoming a wife and then a mother, I developed my own style of cooking, one that is deeply rooted in the flavors of Rome and Southern Italy but is infused with the unique and personal creativity I bring to my kitchen every day.

All of the experiences that came before shaped me into the Pasta Queen you know today. The recipes in this chapter are the ones that I invented after decades of cooking traditional Italian dishes with passion and love, and they feel uniquely mine. Anyone familiar with Italian cuisine will recognize the origins of the dishes in this chapter: They are anchored in the ingredients, techniques, and flavors of Rome and the south of Italy, just like the roots my family planted in the soil so many years ago. But they reimagine the classics or bring a novel technique to a traditional dish to create something new and beautiful.

These dishes are the ones that have defined me as Pasta Queen and that *you* made viral sensations. Allow them to serve as a compass for your own pasta renaissance. As we cook together and work through the lessons in this book, I know you are already on your way to becoming pasta royalty yourself. Whether you have been rolling pasta every Sunday since you could stand, or you've never even boiled a pot of water before, I hope these recipes inspire you and give you the tools to entertain, nourish, and entice your guests—and yourself—with meals that are just gorgeous.

PASTA QUEEN PESTO

PESTO WITH PINE NUTS AND PISTACHIOS

Serves 4

Total prep and cooking time: 15 minutes

Alternate pasta shapes:
eliche, fresh tagliatelle, vesuvi

Sea salt

1 pound linguine

80 grams/3 ounces (4 loosely packed cups fresh basil leaves, plus more for garnish

2 garlic cloves, peeled

60 grams/2 ounces (about ¾ cup) finely grated Pecorino Romano

60 grams/2 ounces (about ¾ cup) finely grated Parmigiano-Reggiano

30 grams/1 ounce (about 3 tablespoons) pine nuts

30 grams/1 ounce (about 3 tablespoons) pistachios

120 grams/4¼ ounces (about ½ cup) extra-virgin olive oil

WATCH THIS RECIPE

Everyone loves the classic electric green pesto from Genova (see Pesto alla Genovese, page 126), a passionate kiss of blended basil, pine nuts, garlic, cheese, and extra-virgin olive oil. My deep Southern Italian roots make me crave something a little different, something that would be absolutely scandalous in Genova and its surrounding villages: pistachios, which add a dynamic depth to the northern classic and even improves it with their earthy nuttiness. Try it for yourself, and—if you dare—tell a native of Genova it's even better than the original.

Bring a large pot of water to a rolling boil over high heat. Season with salt until the water tastes like a seasoned soup. Drop in the pasta and cook until al dente.

Meanwhile, in a food processor, combine the basil leaves, garlic, Pecorino Romano, Parmigiano-Reggiano, pine nuts, pistachios, and olive oil and blend until smooth.

Use a spatula to scrape the pesto into a large bowl.

Transfer the pasta and ¼ cup of pasta cooking water to the bowl with the pesto and toss until each strand is luxuriously draped with the green pesto, adding more water as needed 1 tablespoon at a time to make the sauce silky and luscious.

Serve garnished with fresh basil leaves.

GORGEOUS TIP

You can use any high-quality pistachio you like—I recommend tasting different kinds to see the variety of sweet and savory flavors pistachios can offer—but I love the electric-green, sweetly earthy variety that grows around the village of Bronte on the western slopes of Mt. Etna in Sicily.

LORD LEMONY PESTO

GNOCCHETTI SARDI
WITH LEMON, MINT, AND
PISTACHIOS

Serves 4

Total prep and cooking time:
15 minutes

Alternate pasta shapes:
linguine, fusilli, vesuvi

60 grams/2 ounces
(3 loosely packed cups) fresh mint
leaves, plus more for garnish

50 grams/1¾ ounces (about ½ cup)
pistachios

1 garlic clove, peeled

60 grams/2 ounces (about ¾ cup)
finely grated Pecorino Romano

About 1½ tablespoons fresh lemon
juice, plus grated zest for garnish

60 grams/2 ounces (about ¼ cup)
extra-virgin olive oil

Sea salt

1 pound gnocchetti sardi

Creamy pesto is a fast and delicious sauce that can be made in a little more than a minute and requires nothing more than a food processor to combine the ingredients. I especially love this personal version of pesto. It has an herb, nuts, and cheese in common with Pesto alla Genovese (page 126) and it has a similar twist to Pasta Queen Pesto (page 202) because it uses pistachios, but it has an even more unique ingredient: mint.

Bring a large pot of water to a rolling boil over high heat. Season with salt until the water tastes like seasoned soup. Drop in the pasta and cook until al dente.

Meanwhile, in a food processor, combine the mint, pistachios, garlic, Pecorino Romano, lemon juice, and olive oil and blend until smooth.

Use a spatula to scrape the pesto into a large bowl.

Transfer the gnocchetti sardi to the bowl with the pesto and gently stir the pasta and pesto together, adding pasta cooking water 1 tablespoon at a time as needed to loosen the pesto.

Serve garnished with fresh mint leaves and lemon zest.

GORGEOUS TIP

This pesto is very versatile, and you can make it your own by changing the proportions of mint to pistachios to cheese based on your flavor preferences and what you have in your pantry. That's the fun of pesto: It can be completely personalized, and you can really get creative and make it out of any combination of herbs, nuts, and cheeses you fancy—and all in about a minute, too!

RED PASSION PESTO

SUN-DRIED TOMATO AND ALMOND PESTO

Serves 4

Total prep and cooking time:
15 minutes

Alternate pasta shapes:
eliche giganti, fusilloni,
gnocchetti sardi

1 pound fusilli

60 grams/2 ounces (3 loosely
packed cups) fresh basil leaves,
plus more for garnish

50 grams/1¾ ounces
(5 tablespoons) blanched almonds

1 garlic clove, peeled

60 grams/2 ounces (about ¾ cup)
finely grated Pecorino Romano

60 grams/2 ounces (about ¾ cup)
extra-virgin olive oil

120 grams/4¼ ounces sun-dried
tomatoes, soaked, drained, and
diced

150 grams/5¼ ounces (about 1 cup)
Homemade Ricotta (page 186)
or store-bought fresh ricotta
(I prefer sheep's milk)

Have you ever had the experience of feeling so connected to a place that you felt like you lived there in a past life? When I was a teenager, I spent the summer on the Sicilian island of Panarea and it had that feeling for me. The Sicilians I met were raw, fiery, and affectionate, quick to show love and almost charged by the sun that beat down on their islands. Panarea was instantly welcoming. For three months, I ate the simple olive oil, ricotta, and tomato-rich cuisine cooked by the island's magical people while warm salty sea breezes caressed my skin. When I left, it was like I was leaving home, though I had never even been to Sicily before that. Years later, as a way to remember my time there, I created the red passion pesto: a basil and almond blend spiked with tangy sun-dried tomatoes that are tamed by creamy ricotta. Each bite is a gorgeous reminder of sun-drenched Panarea and its solar-powered flavors.

Bring a large pot of water to a rolling boil over high heat. Season with salt until the water tastes like seasoned soup. Drop in the pasta and cook until al dente.

Meanwhile, in a blender, combine the basil, almonds, garlic, Pecorino Romano, and olive oil and blend until the pesto reaches the consistency you desire—I like a nearly smooth one.

Use a spatula to scrape the pesto into a large bowl, then fold in the sun-dried tomatoes and ricotta. Add a tablespoon of pasta cooking water to loosen the sauce if needed, then add the pasta to the bowl with the pesto and toss with energy and love.

Serve garnished with basil leaves.

GORGEOUS TIP

Soak the sun-dried tomatoes in warm water until they plump, about 10 minutes. Then drain and dice them. Only the most high-powered food processors or blenders can blend them into the pesto. If you have one, you can add the tomatoes with the other ingredients. Otherwise, stir in at the end.

The WHIPPING SICILIAN

SPAGHETTI WITH
GARLIC, CHILI PEPPER,
AND PARSLEY

Serves 4

Total prep and cooking time:
25 minutes

Alternate pasta shapes:
tonnarelli, linguine

Sea salt

1 pound spaghetti

3 garlic cloves, minced

2 to 3 chili peppers (I like cayenne
and Calabrian), thinly sliced

½ cup extra-virgin olive oil

2 tablespoons finely chopped
fresh parsley leaves

120 grams/4¼ ounces
(about 1½ cups) finely grated
Pecorino Romano

WATCH THIS RECIPE

Long ago in the deep south of Italy, raw garlic, chili peppers, and parsley were massaged with powerfully flavorful extra-virgin olive oil, a sprinkle of salt, and a whole lot of passion. The perfumed oil was then mixed off the flame with long spaghetti strands, a splash of tears of the gods, and savory sheep's milk cheese to create a dish that is silky and unforgettable (just like you are). Inspired by this ancient dish called *spaghetti alla carrettiera*, for the Whipping Sicilian I just barely kiss the garlic, chili, and parsley with heat so their flavors stay alive and bright and don't mellow out from too much cooking.

Bring a large pot of water to a rolling boil over high heat. Season with salt until the water tastes like a seasoned soup. Drop in the pasta and cook until al dente.

Meanwhile, in a large deep sauté pan or large bowl (off the heat), combine the garlic, chili peppers, a heavy pinch of salt, the olive oil, and parsley. Let the oil infuse with the flavors and aromas of the garlic, chili, and parsley.

Transfer the pasta to the sauté pan along with 2 tablespoons of pasta cooking water and toss vigorously with the Pecorino Romano, adding more pasta water as needed to make a loose and luscious sauce.

Serve.

The LAZY PRINCESS

CREAMY PEAS

Serves 4

———

Total prep and cooking time:
40 minutes

———

Alternate pasta shapes:
margheritine, lumachine

½ white onion, diced

Sea salt

3 tablespoons extra-virgin olive oil

4 cups (about 1½ pounds) fresh or
frozen peas

Freshly ground black pepper

8 cups boiling water

1 pound ditalini

2 large eggs

60 grams/2 ounces (about ¾ cup)
finely grated Pecorino Romano

60 grams/2 ounces (about ¾ cup)
finely grated Parmigiano-Reggiano,
plus more for dusting

———

WATCH THIS RECIPE

Many years ago, a prince was searching far and wide for a suitable wife but could find no one who rose to his noble status. One rainy night, a stranded, beautiful woman sought refuge in his palace. She was instructed to sleep atop twenty feather mattresses, underneath which the prince's mother had placed a single pea. In the morning, the stranger awoke complaining of a sleepless night. She had felt the pea intensely through the many layers, proving her royal blood.

I was inspired by "The Princess and the Pea" when I created this one-pot dish, a lazy but extremely delicious concoction of creamy peas in which pasta is cooked *pasta minestrata* style (see page xxiii), in the same pot as the simmering pea broth. A princess is perfectly within her rights to be lazy whenever she wants but should never compromise on taste, so use fresh peas in the spring for a velvety masterpiece—frozen peas are a fine substitute out of season. Simmering them gently and seasoning them as they cook will make them even more flavorful. Bind all the flavors together by folding in a savory mixture of eggs and cheese.

In a large pot, sizzle the onion seasoned with a pinch of salt in the olive oil over medium-low heat until the onion becomes slightly translucent and releases all of its flavor into the olive oil, 3 to 4 minutes. Add the peas, another heavy pinch of salt, and a scrunch of black pepper. Pour in 3 to 4 cups of boiling water to cover the peas, increase the heat to medium, and simmer until they are soft, about 8 minutes.

Carefully transfer three-quarters of the peas to a food processor or blender and blend until smooth. Use a spoon to push the puree through a sieve back into the pot with the remaining peas, then add the pasta and 2 cups of boiling water. Cook until the pasta is al dente, adding more boiling water as needed to keep the pasta cooking and the pea broth nice and loose. You may not need all the water.

GORGEOUS TIP

While the pasta cooks, in a small bowl, whisk together the eggs, Pecorino Romano, and Parmigiano-Reggiano.

Remove the pot from the heat and stir the egg/cheese mixture into the pasta to finish this work of art. Serve with Parmigiano-Reggiano dusted on top.

Keep a pot of water boiling next to the pot with the peas. Adding boiling water to the peas and pasta as they cook will help them cook evenly instead of shocking the cooking process with room temperature or cold water.

LEMON TEMPTRESS

SPAGHETTINI COOKED IN LEMON-INFUSED WATER

Serves 4

---

*Total prep and cooking time,
including infusion:
10 hours 25 minutes*

Alternate pasta shapes:
spaghetti, linguine

Peel of 4 large lemons

6 fresh lemon leaves

1 tablespoon extra-virgin olive oil

Sea salt

1 pound spaghettini

80 grams/3 ounces (about 1 cup) grated provolone (I like Provolone del Monaco)

Grated zest of 2 lemons (2 tablespoons)

WATCH THIS RECIPE

The scent of lemons rides on the breeze that caress the streets of Vico Equense, an endearing village en route to the Amalfi Coast. There, a wonderful man named Peppe Guida cooks soulful food at his Michelin-starred restaurant Antica Osteria Nonna Rosa, where he expertly taps into the essence of Italy with every dish. They call Peppe the pasta whisperer, and we became friends instantly. He is just as obsessed with pasta and fresh ingredients as I am, and he has inspired and challenged my cooking so much. For example, I don't usually like spaghettini, the thin strands of pasta also known as angel hair. I prefer the substance and thickness of spaghetti, and the slightly thicker spaghettoni. Yet he convinced me that this dish, which is made by infusing water with the zest and leaves of fresh lemons, calls for the most delicate pasta strand there is. The spaghettini is cooked directly in the lemon infusion, another gorgeous example of the *pasta risottata* technique (see page xxiii), which uses the starch released into the cooking water from the pasta to add a note of creaminess and depth to the sauce that is next level. If you cannot find Provolone del Monaco, use a strongly flavored or aged provolone. The dish calls for richness, and the flavor of a mild provolone would get lost.

In a medium saucepan, bring 6 cups of water just to the edge of a boil over medium-low heat. Add the lemon peel and leaves, then remove from the heat and set aside overnight to infuse the water with the citrus essence.

The next day, strain the lemon-infused water. In a saucepan (with a diameter large enough to accommodate the whole uncooked spaghettini comfortably), combine 4 cups of the lemon-infused water, ½ tablespoon of the olive oil, and a heavy pinch of salt. Bring to a simmer over medium-high heat.

At the same time, in a medium pot, bring the remaining lemon-infused water to a boil over high heat and keep it simmering beside the pan.

recipe continues

GORGEOUS TIPS

Add the spaghettini to the pan with the infused water and olive oil and cook, adding any additional simmering lemon-infused water as needed to cook the pasta until it is al dente.

Remove from the heat. Drizzle with the remaining ½ tablespoon of the olive oil and sprinkle with three-quarters of the grated lemon zest. Add the provolone and stir vigorously to make a thick and creamy sauce.

Serve garnished with the remaining grated lemon zest.

Only use organic, untreated lemons and leaves for this dish, and be sure to only use the zest—the thin colored layer of the peel, which is rich in essential oils—and discard the bitter white pith. Use a very sharp knife or very precise vegetable peeler to remove only the thin outer layer of the peel. If you are lucky enough to have a lemon tree at home, use your own. If you cannot find lemon leaves, omit them and double the amount of zest in the infusion instead.

Dehydrate 2 lemon leaves in either a conventional or microwave oven, and then crumble them with your hands to use as a garnish.

The RISE *of* VENUS

PACCHERI WITH MUSSELS, CLAMS, AND TOMATOES

Serves 4

Total prep and cooking time:
25 minutes

Alternate pasta shapes:
linguine, spaghetti

2 garlic cloves, minced

½ cup extra-virgin olive oil

230 grams/8 ounces grape or cherry tomatoes, halved

Sea salt

2 teaspoons roughly chopped fresh parsley leaves, plus more for garnish

1 cup dry white wine

2 pounds mussels, beards removed and scrubbed

2 pounds small clams (I like Manila or littleneck), cleaned (see How to Clean Clams, page 55)

1 pound paccheri

Venus, the Roman goddess of love, was birthed by the sea, rising out of its churning water to command all that is beautiful in the world. In artwork, she is often shown at the moment of her birth, fully and perfectly formed, riding the surf on a seashell. Like the shells that trim the coastline where she landed, the paccheri pasta in this dish provide the perfect nooks for mussels and clams, which settle into their tubes when combined. The Rise of Venus will make your taste buds burst with flavor.

Bring a large pot of water to a rolling boil over high heat.

Meanwhile, in a large deep sauté pan, cook the garlic in the olive oil over medium-low heat until it starts sizzling with little bubbles around it, 1 to 2 minutes. Add the tomatoes and season with a heavy pinch of salt and the parsley. Sizzle until the tomatoes have softened and are beginning to melt into the oil, about 5 minutes. Increase the heat to medium-high and add the wine, mussels, and clams and cook until the wave of Venus transforms it all into pure beauty. Use tongs to transfer the mussels and clams to a medium bowl as soon as they open. Some will open within 30 seconds, others after about 3 minutes. Discard any mussels or clams that do not open. Pick three-quarters of the clam and mussel meats from their shells, discarding the shells, and set aside. Leave the remaining clams and mussels as is.

Once the water has reached a rolling boil, season with salt until the water tastes like seasoned soup. Drop in the pasta and cook until very al dente (a little more than half the recommended cooking time).

Transfer the paccheri to the sauté pan and fold them into the sauce with the gentle love of Venus. Cook until the sauce reduces and the pasta is al dente, adding more pasta cooking water as needed to cook the pasta. Add all of the cooked mussels and clams back to the pan and toss well to warm them. Serve sprinkled with a flurry of parsley.

The COBBLER'S WIFE

PASTA FOR TWO WITH FRESH
TOMATOES AND CHEESE

Serves 2

Total prep and cooking time:
25 minutes

Alternate pasta shapes:
tonnarelli, fettuccine

Sea salt

8 ounces spaghetti

1 garlic clove, minced

1 fresh chili pepper (I like cayenne
and Calabrian chilies), sliced into
⅛-inch-thick rounds

2 tablespoons extra-virgin olive oil

8 fresh basil leaves, torn, plus whole
leaves for garnish

130 grams/4½ ounces grape
tomatoes, halved

40 grams/1.4 ounces (about ½ cup)
finely grated Parmigiano-Reggiano

40 grams/1.4 ounces (about ½ cup)
finely grated Pecorino Romano

Freshly ground black pepper

WATCH THIS RECIPE

This is a lover's pasta and the ultimate expression of devotion. Long ago, a shoemaker's wife was trying to impress her husband by sizzling garlic, chilies, and basil in extra-virgin olive oil. She then added fresh tomatoes to the pan and bathed them in pasta water until they were soft and shiny. Finally, for the ultimate creaminess, she added a little pasta water and a flurry of Parmigiano-Reggiano and Pecorino Romano cheeses that melted into the sauce, making it irresistible.

Although this is a lover's pasta that's made for two and plated on a large dish for sharing, you can easily scale it up to share your love with a crowd. Adding the basil to the hot oil instead of the tomato sauce—a trick one of my aunts taught me—infuses the oil with its sweet and herbal flavors.

Bring a large pot of water to a rolling boil over high heat. Season with salt until the water tastes like a seasoned soup. Drop in the pasta and cook until very al dente (a little more than half the recommended cooking time).

Meanwhile, in a large deep sauté pan, cook the garlic and chili peppers in the olive oil over medium-low heat until the garlic starts sizzling with little bubbles around it, 1 to 2 minutes. Add the basil leaves and sizzle until fragrant, about 15 seconds. Increase the heat to medium-high, add the tomatoes, season with salt, and spoon over a ladle (½ cup) of pasta cooking water. Cook until the tomatoes are soft but not quite melted into the sauce, about 5 minutes. Add more water as needed to keep the sauce glossy.

Transfer the pasta to the sauté pan along with a ladle (½ cup) of pasta cooking water and cook until the pasta is al dente. Remove from the heat and stir in the Parmigiano-Reggiano and Pecorino Romano, tossing with the passion of an Italian until the sauce is thick and clings to each pasta strand, adding more pasta water as needed to keep the sauce very juicy.

Twirl the pasta into two nests and serve on a single plate garnished with a scrunch of pepper and fresh basil leaves.

GORGEOUS TIP

This is a supremely simple recipe that I only make in the summer when tomatoes are at their peak flavor. With so few simple ingredients, you really must use the best ones you can find. If tomatoes are out of season, use an outrageously high-quality canned tomato brand that is so intense, it practically tastes like it's just been plucked from a vine. Do a blind taste test of various brands to discover your favorite.

LADY *in* PINK

PASTA WITH VODKA SAUCE AND SHRIMP

Serves 4

———

Total prep and cooking time:
30 minutes

———

Alternate pasta shape:
ziti

1 shallot, diced

1 garlic clove, minced

Sea salt

3 tablespoons extra-virgin olive oil

¼ cup tomato paste

1 cup vodka

1 (14.5-ounce) can whole peeled tomatoes, crushed by hand (see page 58)

1 cup heavy cream

Freshly ground black pepper

1 teaspoon chili flakes or 1 fresh chili pepper (I like cayenne and Calabrian chilies)

¾ pound medium shrimp, peeled and deveined (see page 148)

1 pound penne

2 teaspoons roughly chopped fresh parsley leaves, plus more for garnish

Something amazing happens when you sizzle shallots and garlic in extra-virgin olive oil, then intensify it with tomato paste and spike it with vodka. Then add a bit of heavy cream to mingle with the acidity of the tomatoes and make a luscious pink sauce that on its own would make a sailor blush. But there's more. Tender shrimp and chili flakes added without remorse will jump-start your taste buds and have you wondering if you really want to share.

I invented this dish as a way to spice up—literally—*penne alla vodka* and make it feel more grown-up with the addition of succulent shrimp. The Lady in Pink is all about managing the shrimp, sauce, and pasta so they all finish cooking at the same time. Fresh medium shrimp will turn pink and cook through in a rapidly simmering sauce in about 2½ minutes; larger shrimp will take a bit longer.

Bring a large pot of water to a rolling boil over high heat.

Meanwhile, in a large deep sauté pan, cook the shallot, garlic, and a pinch of salt in the olive oil over medium-low heat until they start sizzling with little bubbles around them, 1 to 2 minutes. Add the tomato paste, increase the heat to medium-high, and stir to envelop the shallots and garlic in the intense tomato flavor. Fry until the tomato paste turns a brick hue, about 2 minutes. Add the vodka and simmer until the alcohol aroma evaporates and the liquid reduces by half, about 1½ minutes. Add the tomatoes and cream and season with salt and a scrunch of black pepper, stirring to combine. Simmer, stirring frequently, for 5 minutes to perfectly mingle the flavors and thicken the sauce. Add the chili and shrimp and cook just until they are cooked through and pink, about 2½ minutes.

Once the water has reached a rolling boil, season with salt until the water tastes like a seasoned soup. Drop in the pasta and cook until al dente.

Meanwhile, carefully ladle half the sauce into a food processor or blender and blend until smooth, bringing to life all the intense flavors. Return the sauce to the sauté pan and bring back to a simmer.

Transfer the pasta to the sauté pan and toss until thoroughly coated. Remove from the heat and stir in the parsley. Add a tablespoon or two of the pasta cooking water if needed to thin out the sauce until it is sultry and creamy. Season with salt to taste. Serve garnished with parsley.

MINTY MISTRESS

FOUR-CHEESE PASTA
WITH MINT

Serves 4

Total prep and cooking time:
25 minutes

Alternate pasta shapes:
ziti, penne lisce

Sea salt

1 pound lumache

2 tablespoons unsalted butter

1 cup heavy cream

60 grams/2 ounces provolone, cut
into ½-inch cubes

60 grams/2 ounces Fontina, cut
into ½-inch cubes

60 grams/2 ounces Gruyère, cut
into ½-inch cubes

½ teaspoon freshly grated nutmeg

Freshly ground black pepper

60 grams/2 ounces (about ¾ cup)
finely grated Parmigiano-Reggiano

2 teaspoons roughly chopped fresh
mint leaves, plus more for garnish

Italy is no stranger to buttery cheese pasta recipes, especially in the north. The Mistress takes things a step further and melts a mixture of decadent cheeses into cream before adding the unique twist of aromatic mint. The salty provolone, sweet Fontina, and funky Gruyère all blend into one another in their creamy glory, then a pinch of nutmeg and a scrunch of pepper elevate the cheese flavors to make this dish next-level (just like you are). The mint cuts the richness of the cheese, while adding a bit of freshness. Parmigiano-Reggiano and the tears of the gods bring it all together to create a gorgeous sauce that flows gently into each contour of the pasta's curves.

Bring a large pot of water to a rolling boil over high heat. Season with salt until the water tastes like a seasoned soup. Drop in the pasta and cook until al dente.

Meanwhile, in a large deep sauté pan, melt the butter over medium heat. Drizzle in the cream and cook, stirring frequently, until the mixture thickens, about 5 minutes. Add the cheeses one at a time in this order: provolone, Fontina, and Gruyère, letting each cheese melt before adding the next. Add the grated nutmeg and a scrunch of pepper.

Transfer the pasta to the sauté pan, adding pasta cooking water a tablespoon at a time as needed to loosen the sauce. Remove from the heat and stir in the Parmigiano-Reggiano and fresh mint.

Serve garnished with fresh mint and a scrunch of pepper.

GODDESS *of* LOVE

❦

TORTELLINI WITH PEAS, PROSCIUTTO, AND CREAM

Serves 4

———

Total prep and cooking time:
25 minutes

———

Alternate pasta shape:
ravioli

¼ cup extra-virgin olive oil

1 shallot, minced

Sea salt

1 cup fresh or frozen peas
(if using fresh, cook in salted water
until tender, about 2 minutes)

Freshly ground black pepper

2 tablespoons unsalted butter

6 slices (about 5 ounces)
Prosciutto di Parma, cut into
1 × ¼ × ¼-inch sticks

1 cup heavy cream

60 grams

60 grams/2 ounces (about ¾ cup)
finely grated Parmigiano-Reggiano,
plus more for dusting

Tortellini (page 21), Tortelloni
(page 23), or 1 pound store-bought
fresh tortellini

Legend has it that the shape of tortellini was inspired by the belly button of Venus, the Roman goddess of love. Venus was traveling to cast her spells on unsuspecting lovers, and she spent a night at an inn in Northern Italy. The innkeeper couldn't resist her beauty and spied on her as she undressed. He saw her seductive belly button through the keyhole of her bedroom door and swore to create a pasta shape that was just as beautiful. Tortellini were born in the innkeeper's kitchen.

As an offering to Venus, I sizzle shallots in extra-virgin olive oil with peas, butter, prosciutto, and heavy cream to make a godlike cloak for the tortellini. Choose classic tortellini—the traditional meaty version—or a seasoned ricotta filling in the slightly larger tortelloni to satisfy your own inner love goddess.

Bring a large pot of water to a rolling boil over high heat.

Meanwhile, in a large deep sauté pan, heat the olive oil and shallots over low heat. Season with salt and sizzle until soft, about 5 minutes. Add the peas, a heavy pinch of salt, and a scrunch of black pepper. Melt in the butter, scatter in the prosciutto, and pour in the cream. Increase the heat to medium-high and cook, stirring frequently, until the sauce thickens and coats the back of a spoon, about 5 minutes. Stir in the Parmigiano-Reggiano.

Once the water has reached a rolling boil, season with salt until the water tastes like seasoned soup. Drop in the pasta and cook until the tortellini float and are tender, 2 to 3 minutes.

Gently transfer the tortellini to the cream sauce with the tenderness of Venus. Swirl gently to bathe in the sauce, loosening it with pasta cooking water as needed.

Serve dusted with Parmigiano-Reggiano.

The SNAPPY HARLOT

PASTA WITH OLIVES,
ANCHOVIES, CAPERS, AND
CALABRIAN CHILI PASTE

Serves 4

Total prep and cooking time:
25 minutes

Alternate pasta shapes:
spaghettoni, linguine

2 garlic cloves, minced

¼ cup extra-virgin olive oil

½ cup olives (I like Gaeta or
Kalamata), rinsed and pitted

2 tablespoons capers
(rinsed and soaked if salt-packed,
drained if in brine)

2 anchovy fillets (rinsed and soaked
if salt-packed, drained if in oil)

1 (28-ounce) can whole
peeled tomatoes, crushed by hand
(see page 58)

Sea salt

1 tablespoon Calabrian chili paste

1 pound spaghetti

Coarsely chopped fresh parsley
leaves, for garnish

Calabrian chilies, for garnish
(optional)

The Snappy Harlot builds on the foundation of Puttanesca (page 68). It recalls the ladies of the night that may have inspired the timeless classic, and the potent pasta dishes spiked with garlic and chilies they made to fuel their passion. But this recipe adds Calabrian chili paste, a tangy and slightly hot aphrodisiac, taking the sauce to a spice level that will dare you not to break into a sweat as you twirl your spaghetti.

In a large deep sauté pan, cook the garlic in the olive oil over medium-low heat until the garlic starts sizzling with little bubbles around it, 1 to 2 minutes. Add the olives, capers, and anchovies and cook until the anchovies have melted into the oil, infusing the other ingredients with their seductive savoriness, about 2 minutes. Add the tomatoes, season with salt, and increase the heat to medium-high. Stir in the Calabrian chili paste and simmer just until the tomatoes lose their raw flavor and the sauce begins to concentrate, about 8 minutes.

Meanwhile, bring a large pot of water to a rolling boil over high heat. Season with salt until the water tastes like a seasoned soup. Drop in the pasta and cook until very al dente (a little more than half the recommended cooking time).

Transfer the pasta to the sauté pan along with a ladle (½ cup) of pasta cooking water and toss until it clings to the pasta strands. Cook the pasta in the sauce until al dente. Check frequently to see when the pasta is done and add more pasta cooking water as needed to finish cooking the pasta and keep the sauce loose.

Serve garnished with parsley and a whole Calabrian chili (if using).

The REBELLIOUS CARBONARA

VEGETARIAN CARBONARA
WITH FRIED ZUCCHINI, EGG,
PECORINO ROMANO, AND
BLACK PEPPER

Serves 4

Total prep and cooking time:
30 minutes

¼ cup plus 1 tablespoon extra-virgin
olive oil

4 medium zucchini, cut into
⅛-inch-thick coins

4 large egg yolks

60 grams/2 ounces (about ¾ cup)
finely grated Pecorino Romano, plus
more for garnish

1½ teaspoons freshly ground black
pepper, plus more for garnish

Sea salt

1 pound spaghetti

WATCH THIS RECIPE

This carbonara made with fried zucchini instead of guanciale is a rule breaker. Carbonara (page 39) is practically a religion in Rome, and a vegetarian version like this one might set off a furious debate among pasta purists. But I know that even the most skeptical carbonara lover will be a convert after just one bite of this spaghetti dripping in a soft and silky egg and pecorino sauce. To compensate for the absence of the guanciale in this dish, I've added something equally tantalizing: zucchini coins sizzled in oil until golden. Zucchini carbonara is my perfect substitute for the rich and fatty original.

Bring a large pot of water to a rolling boil over high heat.

Meanwhile, in a large deep sauté pan, heat the oil over medium-low heat until it begins to shimmer. Add the zucchini coins and stir to coat them evenly in the oil. Cook, turning with tongs if necessary, until shiny and golden, about 5 minutes. Remove from the heat. Set aside one-quarter of the fried coins to drain on a paper towel to be used as a garnish. Set the pan with the remaining zucchini aside.

In a bowl, combine the egg yolks, Pecorino Romano, pepper, and reserved zucchini and stir passionately to make a thick and creamy sauce. Add 2 tablespoons of boiling water to the mixture and mix energetically to temper the eggs.

Once the water has reached a rolling boil, season with salt until the water tastes like a seasoned soup. Drop in the pasta and cook until al dente.

Transfer the pasta to the pan you cooked the zucchini in. Stir to coat in the oil, then add the egg and zucchini mixture and a splash (¼ cup) of pasta cooking water, stirring vigorously. Set the pan over low heat and toss energetically to combine, adding more pasta water if needed to make the sauce creamy and to coat the pasta.

Serve garnished with the reserved zucchini coins and with a scrunch of pepper on top.

The ANGRY BARONESS

HOT AND SPICY VODKA
CREAM SAUCE WITH TROFIE

Serves 4

Total prep and cooking time:
25 minutes

Alternate pasta shapes:
gigli, cavatelli, fusilli

2 garlic cloves, minced

1 small red onion, diced

Sea salt

¼ cup extra-virgin olive oil

¼ cup plus 2 tablespoons tomato
paste

1 cup vodka

1 tablespoon chili flakes

1 cup heavy cream

Freshly ground black pepper

1 tablespoon unsalted butter

60 grams/2 ounces (about ¾ cup)
finely grated Parmigiano-Reggiano

1 pound trofie

Fresh parsley leaves, for garnish

WATCH THIS RECIPE

The Angry Baroness builds on the flavors of Penne all'Arrabbiata (page 49) and pairs them with an alluring and creamy vodka sauce. She's sassy yet classy and her only vice is spice. Spiking the tomato vodka cream sauce with chili flakes creates a chemical reaction of love and really brings the heat. The chilies' deep and persistent fire will awaken your senses, while a little butter will cool your palate so it's eager for the next bite.

Bring a large pot of water to a rolling boil over high heat.

Meanwhile, in a large deep sauté pan, sizzle the garlic, onion, and a pinch of salt in the olive oil over medium-low heat until the onion becomes slightly translucent and releases all of its flavors into the olive oil, 3 to 4 minutes. Add the tomato paste, increase the heat to medium-high, and stir to envelop the garlic and onions in the intense tomato flavor. Fry until it turns a brick hue, about 2 minutes. Add the vodka and simmer until the alcohol aroma evaporates and the liquid reduces by half, about 1½ minutes. Add the chili flakes and sizzle until fragrant, about 15 seconds. Once the chili has infused the intensely flavored mixture, add the cream to bring it all together. Season with salt and scrunch of black pepper and stir frequently to continue marrying the flavors while the sauce thickens, about 5 minutes. Stir in the butter and Parmigiano-Reggiano.

Once the water has reached a rolling boil, season with salt until the water tastes like a seasoned soup. Drop in the pasta and cook until al dente.

Transfer the pasta to the sauté pan along with a tablespoon of pasta cooking water, fold in the pasta and massage until the sauce drapes each piece in its powerful flavors.

Serve garnished with parsley.

LEMON RICOTTA DELIGHT

ELICHE WITH CREAMY
RICOTTA AND LEMON

Serves 4

Total prep and cooking time:
45 minutes

Alternate pasta shapes:
conchigliette, gemelli, fusilli

Sea salt

1 pound eliche

1 pound Homemade Ricotta
(page 186) or store-bought fresh
ricotta (I like sheep's milk)

Grated zest of 2 lemons
and the juice of 1 lemon, plus more
zest for garnish

Freshly ground black pepper

4 to 6 fresh basil leaves,
torn, plus more fresh leaves for
garnish

60 grams/2 ounces (about ¾ cup)
finely grated Pecorino Romano

WATCH THIS RECIPE

Lemon Ricotta Delight is a reminder that pasta is whatever you want it to be, and you don't have to feel limited by what feels traditional. Instead, be inspired by what is fresh and delicious near you. Lemons and ricotta were a huge part of my childhood—fragrant citrus is the calling card of Campania, while sheep's milk ricotta is a Roman staple—so I combined them to make this absolutely delicious, no-cook sauce when I was living in London during my early years with Brook. This is one of my most viral recipes on TikTok, and I believe that's because it's fresh and surprising—not to mention fast, so you have more time to gaze into the eyes of your lover over dinner. For this Pasta Queen original, I use gorgeous Florida citrus, stirring together juice and zest with ricotta that I make myself, gently coaxing them into a soft and creamy mixture that coat the curlicue eliche. The ricotta's silkiness and the lemon's tangy acidity create a direct flight to sun-drenched Italy.

Bring a large pot of water to a rolling boil over high heat. Season with salt until the water tastes like a seasoned soup. Drop in the pasta and cook until al dente.

Meanwhile, in a large bowl, combine the ricotta, a splash (¼ cup) of the tears of the gods, lemon zest, and lemon juice. Season with a heavy pinch of salt and a scrunch of pepper.

Fold in the cooked pasta, basil, and Pecorino Romano, adding more pasta water as needed to help the sauce bind to the pasta.

Serve garnished with more lemon zest and basil and a scrunch of pepper.

RED SENSATION

GLUTEN- AND OIL-FREE
PASTA WITH TOMATOES,
PEPPERS, CAPERS,
AND OLIVES

Serves 4

———

Total prep and cooking time:
25 minutes

———

Alternate pasta shape:
gluten-free farfalle

½ red onion, diced

Sea salt

2 small red bell peppers, cut into
¼-inch-wide strips

1 sprig fresh oregano, picked, plus
more for garnish

2 tablespoons capers
(rinsed and soaked if salt-packed,
drained if in brine)

½ cup olives (I like Gaeta and
Kalamata), pitted and halved
lengthwise

1 (18.6-ounce) jar Pomodorini
del Piennolo del Vesuvio or
1¼ (14.5-ounce) cans whole peeled
tomatoes, crushed by hand
(see page 58)

1 pound brown rice penne

Calabrian chile oil, for drizzling
(optional)

This surprising recipe requires no oil! Cooking onions and bell peppers in a splash of water releases their inner essence and fills the entire kitchen with the aromas of love. The addition of fresh oregano, capers, and olives conspire to transport your kitchen to Campania, a journey that is infused with the flavors of special teardrop-shaped tomatoes called Pomodorini del Piennolo del Vesuvio, which are grown on the slopes of Mount Vesuvius. They create an explosion of flavor that walks a dangerous line between sweet and tangy. Adding gluten-free pasta made from brown rice flour completes this healthy meal that doesn't compromise on flavor.

Bring a large pot of water to a rolling boil over high heat.

Meanwhile, in a large deep sauté pan, sizzle the onion with a splash (¼ cup) of water over medium-low heat. Shower with a pinch of salt and cook, stirring frequently, until the onion becomes slightly translucent and releases all of its flavor into the water, 3 to 4 minutes, adding more water as needed to soften the onion. Add the bell peppers and cook just until soft, about 5 minutes, adding water a tablespoon at a time as needed. Stir in the oregano, capers, and olives. Stir in the tomatoes, season with a light shower of salt, then increase the heat to high and cook until the flavors unite and the tomatoes have lost their raw edge, about 5 minutes.

Once the water has reached a rolling boil, season with salt until the water tastes like a seasoned soup. Drop in the pasta and cook until al dente.

Transfer the pasta to the sauté pan along with a tablespoon of pasta cooking water and fold the pasta gently into the sauce.

Serve garnished with fresh oregano and a drizzle of Calabrian chile oil (if using).

GREEN TEMPTATION

FUSILLI WITH CREAMY BROCCOLI, KALE, AND SPINACH

Serves 4

Total prep and cooking time:
25 minutes

Alternate pasta shape:
farfalle

Sea salt

½ pound broccoli florets, separated

½ pound kale leaves stripped from their stems and midribs, roughly chopped

½ pound spinach

1 pound fusilli

1 cup heavy cream

60 grams/2 ounces (about ¾ cup) finely grated Parmigiano-Reggiano, plus more for dusting

Freshly ground black pepper

For about a year while I was living in the UK, I tried juicing. I'd make a vegetable nutrient bomb of spinach, kale, and broccoli rabe with a squeeze of lemon. Although I didn't mind it, there was no chance of getting my kids to try it. *"Basta mamma,"* they'd say, sticking out their tongues whenever I offered it. I came up with this Green Temptation pasta recipe as a solution and haven't looked back since!

Bring a large pot of water to a rolling boil over high heat. Season with salt until the water tastes like a seasoned soup. Working in batches, one vegetable at a time, cook the broccoli, kale, and spinach until soft and tender: about 3 minutes each for the broccoli and kale and 1 minute for the spinach. As they are done, remove the greens with a slotted spoon or a spider strainer and set them aside on a baking sheet to cool. (Reserve the pot of water to cook the pasta.) Reserve a bit of broccoli and kale for garnish.

When the greens are cooled, transfer them and a few tablespoons of cooking water to a food processor or blender and blend until smooth.

Bring the pot of vegetable cooking water back to a rolling boil. Drop in the pasta and cook until al dente.

Meanwhile, in a large deep sauté pan, heat the cream and Parmigiano-Reggiano over medium-high heat. Simmer, stirring frequently, until the cream thickens, about 5 minutes. Stir in the blended greens. Season with salt and a scrunch of pepper.

Transfer the pasta to the sauté pan along with a tablespoon of pasta cooking water. Simmer to marry the flavors and concentrate the sauce.

Serve garnished with the reserved broccoli and kale and dusted with a flurry of Parmigiano-Reggiano.

CREAMY BROCCOLI DELIGHT

ONE-POT CREAMY
BROCCOLI AND PASTA

Serves 4

Total prep and cooking time:
40 minutes

Alternate pasta shapes:
conchigliette, ditali

6 cups Homemade Vegetable Broth
(page 115) or water

1 whole garlic clove, peeled

1 fresh chili pepper (I like cayenne
and Calabrian chilies), thinly sliced

3 tablespoons extra-virgin olive oil

1½ pounds broccoli, separated into
florets, stalk cut into 1-inch pieces

Sea salt

1 pound ditalini

2 large eggs

60 grams/2 ounces (about ¾ cup)
finely grated Pecorino Romano

60 grams/2 ounces (about ¾ cup)
finely grated Parmigiano-Reggiano

Freshly ground black pepper

Broccoli is sweet, earthy, and bitter, and it's one of my favorite ingredients ever. When I cook with it, I want its incredible flavor to infuse the other ingredients. I created this creamy broccoli delight to do just that, blending a portion to make the texture smooth. Then, I add pasta and hot liquid to the broccoli mixture using the *pasta minestrata* method (see page xxiii), cooking until the pasta is done and has totally absorbed the broccoli's essence. The final touch is to mix in eggs and a bit of cheese to beautifully thicken this one-pot meal that is gorgeously green and stunningly delicious.

In a saucepan, bring the vegetable broth to a boil and keep it hot while you cook the broccoli.

In a large pot, heat the garlic and chili pepper in the olive oil over low heat until bubbles form around the garlic, 1 to 2 minutes. Add the broccoli, a heavy pinch of salt, and a splash (¼ cup) broth. Cover and cook until the broccoli is soft, about 6 minutes.

Carefully transfer one-quarter of the broccoli to a bowl and set aside. Use an immersion blender right in the pot to blend the broccoli until smooth (or transfer the broccoli to a food processor to blend and then return the puree to the pot).

Add the pasta and another 1 cup of boiling broth to the pot. Cook until the pasta is al dente, adding more boiling broth as needed. You may not need all the broth.

Meanwhile, in a small bowl, whisk together the eggs, Pecorino Romano, and Parmigiano-Reggiano.

Remove the pot from the heat and stir the egg mixture into the pasta with love.

Serve with a scrunch of pepper and crowned with the reserved broccoli while whispering, "Just gorgeous."

GORGEOUS TIP

Keep the vegetable broth or
water boiling in a pot next to
the broccoli. Adding boiling
liquid will cook the pasta
more consistently than room
temperature liquid, which would
stop or slow the cooking.

CIBUM AMOR EST
Food is love.

This is just the beginning of our pasta journey together.

Every recipe herein is a reflection of my heart, which I have shared so you can paint something magical on your own canvas called life. From building families to creating empires and the making of queens—all of these things have been forged over great food and with great people. The possibilities for what you'd like to create, using fresh and simple food as your inspiration, are endless.

If there is anything I'd like you to take away from this book, it is that you and I are very special. Our journey of experiences is a fascinating story worth telling, despite sometimes feeling tired and beaten by the hits life gives. Look closely, and you will see incredible people who have shared some of the same struggles that you have, who are all unique and interesting. They are important, they feel things, and they care. If we push ourselves to focus on the special qualities of others, and make sure they know they are special, we can slowly start a new renaissance of living—one built around the love that good provides.

Next time you look in the mirror, tell yourself how beautiful, amazing, strong, and courageous you are. Do this often enough and you *will* be, even if you don't feel like you are now. When you go into your next meeting, buy groceries, or speak to a friend, take a pause and admire how everyone you meet has pushed themselves to be better.

Great food and ingredients are how we connect, love, and share ourselves with others. The rewards we seek in life are not just money, status, and fame. These things are nice, but if you look closely, the greatest moments come about when you experience gratitude, love, appreciation, and the accomplishment of creating—and sharing—something wonderful with those around you.

Take any of the pasta recipes in this book and create your own special moments. Look ahead! There is a wonderful life to be had.

Stay gorgeous!

FROM NADIA

FROM *the* PASTA QUEEN, WITH LOVE

This book is first and foremost an acknowledgment of my followers on social media. We have been on a journey together since March 2020 and have shared each other's homes through wonderful pasta recipes. Thank you so much for becoming part of my family. Next, I'd humbly like to thank myself. I believed in myself when The Pasta Queen was just an idea and have never looked back. To Brook, my husband and best friend, I forgive you for doubting me and worrying a little when I told you I was going to do this full time. I know you love me and you've always been there for me, but you are as British as can be and view the world a little more cautiously than I do. In the end, we did it! I want to thank my dad, Tonino, aka Papone. You have always been my number one fan and pushed me to be and do whatever I dreamed of. Next, my brother, Agostino, aka Pasta Bro, you are my right hand, my comedic sous-chef, and so incredible and hardworking. Thank you for the eighteen-hour days of cooking support and endless fights over ingredient quantities. I value that. I also want to thank all the powerful women who have raised me with good values and so much care: Nonna Caterina, Zia Stella, Zia Maria, Zia Pina, Angela, and Michelina. You all have been instrumental in the creation of this book. To my mother, Kathleen, who showed me how to work hard. You were tough, but I know you love me unconditionally. To all my family members who lent their beauty for the photo shoots in the book: It was your first time modeling and you slayed it—especially my great uncle, Zio Franco, who was the star and stole the show. Thank you to my cousin Raffaele, who helped by bringing dozens of freshly made buffalo *mozzarelle* and wine for all of us to enjoy. Katie Parla, you have been truly instrumental in creating this book. I experienced your adventure of enrichment and knowledge unsurpassed by anyone. I want to thank my agency, CAA. I am blessed to have a loving and caring team (Rachel O'Brien, you are amazing). To my literary agent, Brandi Bowles, you have been so supportive and pushed me to put myself out there and write that first book proposal! Kyle and Clayton, my managers, I absolutely love you and I am grateful we found each other; you have brought sanity to the madness. And to the team at Scale Management, you are brilliant and always have my back. I want to thank my editor, Molly Gregory. You are so good at leading me patiently through the process and making sure every little detail is just right, and are always ready to take my calls at any time of day! To my designer, Laura Palese: You understood my design ideas right away and were able to translate them beautifully into a *just gorgeous* cookbook. Food stylist extraordinaire, Alice Adams Carosi: Your sense of aesthetics and your amazing ability to find precious ceramics at the *mercatini* (flea markets) made the pasta itself feel beautiful. To Giovanna Di Lisciandro, my amazing food photographer, I adore you. I can't believe how talented you are, and the passion you put into your work shows through. Thank you to the food styling assistants and cooks, Elisabetta Busini and Giulia Picardo. Veronica Paolillo, I am so thankful you let us raid your kitchen and shoot at the last minute. To my lifestyle photographer, Stef Galea, I have no words . . . The moment I saw your work I had no doubt we were the perfect match. You took what was previously only in my mind and captured it in pictures that I will cherish forever. Only a true artist can do that. Thank you to Delfo, a brilliant assistant who carried us every step of the way. To my book tour producer, Alison Ercolani, I am still in stitches about our crazy tour of the Amalfi Coast and getting lost on streets too dangerous to even explain. To my beauty team, stylist Valentina Fuela and makeup artist Tiziana Porrazzo: You girls made me look and feel like a queen every day we spent together, always there as my cheerleaders and laughing until it hurt. To my amazing illustrator, Dorota: You created gorgeous illustrations that added so much more beauty to the book. To Erika Martini, one of my best friends: Thank you for always being there for me. A huge thank-you to Chef Peppe Guida. I feel that in you I have met my pasta soul mate. Your style of cooking combines hundreds of years of culinary knowledge with your poetry added to it. To Giuseppe Di Martino and his dream team, Maria Teresa Caiazzo and Vale Santonastaso: Thank you so much for the loving help and support in making this book. The pasta gods have blessed your crops to create some of the most gorgeous and tasty pasta in the world. Thank you to Trecca, the family-run trattoria in Rome: You have been so generous in putting up with all of us taking over your place and letting me stand on your tables for hours while shooting pasta! Thank you to Maccheroni restaurant for letting us go wild in your kitchen, and to Er Pantera for serving us endless delicious classic Roman pasta dishes. Cantina Ripagrande, thank you for letting us overwhelm you with a hundred people in one photo shoot! Thank you to Annie from Scooter Rome Tours for letting us play with your vintage Vespas around Rome!

I want to thank all the family-run trattorias that have changed the way I cook forever: Checco er Carettiere, Osteria dei Pontefici, Taverna dei Quaranta, and countless other holes-in-the-wall in Rome that have fed my imagination and shaped the Pasta Queen. I want to thank Agriturismo La Colombaia and their staff, who run the most amazing farm accommodations. You hosted us as if we were family and fed us the most gorgeous foods from your land in the Campania Felix. And last but definitely not least, to Jessica Thomas, my assistant and friend: You're tireless and I appreciate you. You survived our endless late nights in Italy with minimal scars and refused to stop even when I asked you to take a break.

And finally, thank you to the Pasta Gods for making all this possible.

Just gorgeous.

RESOURCES

Cheeses, Cured Meats, and Pantry Items

ALMA GOURMET
almagourmet.com/store
For Italian cheeses, meats, truffles, pasta, extra-virgin olive oil, flour, and pantry items

CAPUTO BROTHERS CREAMERY
caputobrotherscreamery.com
Fresh ricotta and mozzarella curds (if you want to try stretching your own mozzarella)

DI BRUNO BROS.
dibruno.com
Pecorino Romano, Parmigiano-Reggiano, sheep's-milk ricotta, mozzarella, and other Italian cheeses, as well as guanciale

D'ITALIA
ditalia.com
Pastas, oil, cheeses, flour, and pantry items

DOLCETERRA
dolceterra.com
Imported Italian cheeses, sweets, liquors, and pantry items

DOMENICA FIORE
domenicafiore.com
Extra-virgin olive oil from Umbria

LA DEVOZIONE
ladevozionenyc.com
Pastificio Di Martino's online pasta shop offers 126 pasta shapes

GUSTIAMO
gustiamo.com
The finest imported Italian pastas, tomatoes, flour, olive oils, anchovies, capers, and more

MARKET HALL FOODS
markethallfoods.com
Salted anchovies and a wide range of Italian specialty products

ZINGERMAN'S
zingermans.com
Guanciale, cheeses, and a huge variety of Italian specialty products

Nadia's Favorite Dried Pasta Brands

BENEDETTO CAVALIERI
benedettocavalieri.it
Dried durum wheat pasta made in Puglia since 1918

FAELLA
pastificiofaella.it
Pasta maker in Gragnano producing dried pasta shapes since 1907

GENTILE
pastificiogentile.com
Making pasta in Gragnano since 1976

MANCINI
pastamancini.com
Pasta made with wheat grown in Le Marche

PASTAIO VIA CORTA
pastaioviacorta.com
Artisan dried pasta made in Gloucester, Massachusetts, from local organic heirloom wheat varieties

PASTIFICIO DI MARTINO
pastadimartino.it
Dried pasta made in Gragnano since 1912

PASTIFICIO DEI CAMPI
pastificiodeicampi.it
Designer dried pasta made with traceable wheat in Gragnano

SEMOLINA ARTISANAL PASTA
semolinapasta.com
Small-batch dried pasta made in Pasadena, California

SETARO
setaro.it
Dried pasta made in Torre Annunziata since 1939

Nadia's Favorite Gluten-Free Pasta Brands

CASA RUSTICHELLA
casarustichella.com
Abruzzo-based pasta maker with a gluten-free line

JOVIAL
jovialfoods.com
Artisan-crafted, organic pasta in gluten-free and grain-free varieties

NADIA'S FAVORITE
KITCHEN ACCESSORIES,
PASTA TOOLS, AND MORE

PASTA INSPO *by* CATEGORY

INDEX

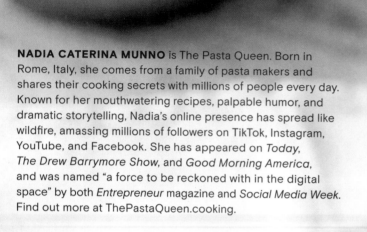

NADIA CATERINA MUNNO is The Pasta Queen. Born in Rome, Italy, she comes from a family of pasta makers and shares their cooking secrets with millions of people every day. Known for her mouthwatering recipes, palpable humor, and dramatic storytelling, Nadia's online presence has spread like wildfire, amassing millions of followers on TikTok, Instagram, YouTube, and Facebook. She has appeared on *Today*, *The Drew Barrymore Show*, and *Good Morning America*, and was named "a force to be reckoned with in the digital space" by both *Entrepreneur* magazine and *Social Media Week*. Find out more at ThePastaQueen.cooking.

KATIE PARLA is a Rome-based *New York Times* bestselling cookbook author, food and beverage journalist, culinary guide, educator, and Emmy-nominated television host. She has written, edited, or contributed to more than thirty books and cohosts *Gola*, a podcast about Italian food and beverage culture. Keep up with Katie on social media @katieparla.